PACEMAKER® PRACTICAL ARITHMETIC SERIES

Money Makes Sense

FOURTH EDITION

by Charles H. Kahn and J. Bradley Hanna

A PACEMAKER® BOOK

Fearon/Janus/Quercus
Belmont, California

Simon & Schuster Education Group

PACEMAKER® PRACTICAL ARITHMETIC SERIES

Money Makes Sense

Using Dollars and Sense

Working Makes Sense

Buying with Sense

Career Math Makes Sense

Cover Photographer: Michael Falconer Photography
Illustrators: Teresa Camozzi and Sam Masami Daijogo

ISBN 0-8224-4518-2

Printed in the United States of America

2.9 8 7 6 5 4
CO

Money Makes Sense!

Does money make sense to you? It should. You will be using money as long as you live. Most people use money almost every day.

You use money when you shop.

You use money when you eat out.

You use money to pay your bills.

You use money when you travel.

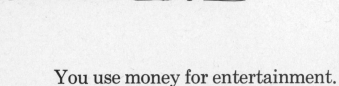

You use money for entertainment.

There are other times when you will use money, too. It makes sense to learn all you can about money.

In this book you will learn about United States money. You will study our coins and dollar bill and get to know them very well. You will soon be able to tell one coin from another quickly. You will also find out how much the different coins are worth. This is the first step in learning how to count money. After a lot of practice, you will know how to count coins and bills correctly.

While you are learning about money, you will also be learning arithmetic. By the time you finish this book, you will know how to add numbers. This will help you in school and outside of school, too.

By using this book, you will see how money makes sense. Your teacher will give you all the help you need. And you will find that learning about money is fun, too!

NAME ____________________

Pretest I

Draw a line from each name to the coin it names.

dime

dollar

quarter

nickel

penny

half-dollar

one cent

ten cents

one dollar

twenty-five cents

five cents

fifty cents

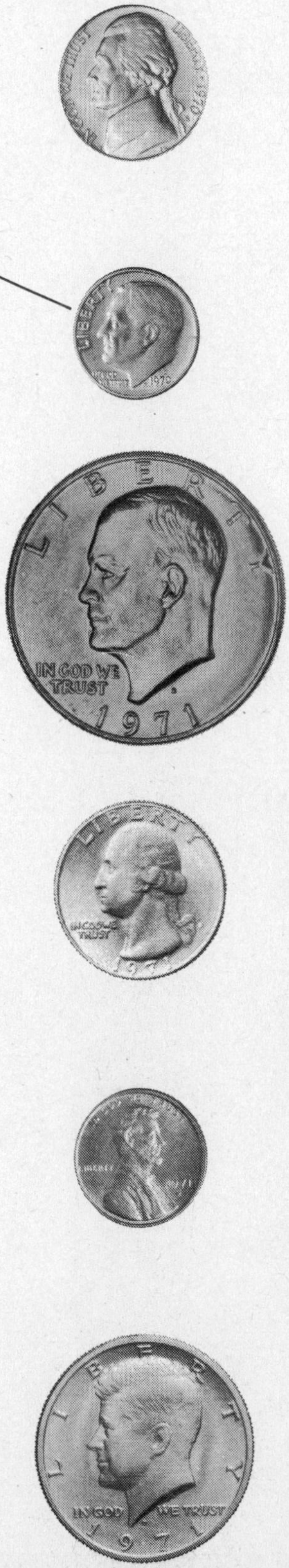

Draw a line from each name to the coin it names.

twenty-five cents

penny

five cents

half-dollar

ten cents

quarter

dime

dollar

fifty cents

nickel

one dollar

one cent

Pretest II

Find the value of each group of coins on the left. Draw a
line under the amount on the right that is equal to the
value of the coins on the left.

1.    =   5 cents
15 cents
<u>10 cents</u>

2.    =   6 cents
11 cents
15 cents

3.    =   30 cents
45 cents
50 cents

4.    =   50 cents
26 cents
35 cents

5.    =   50 cents
75 cents
60 cents

6.    =   80 cents
60 cents
35 cents

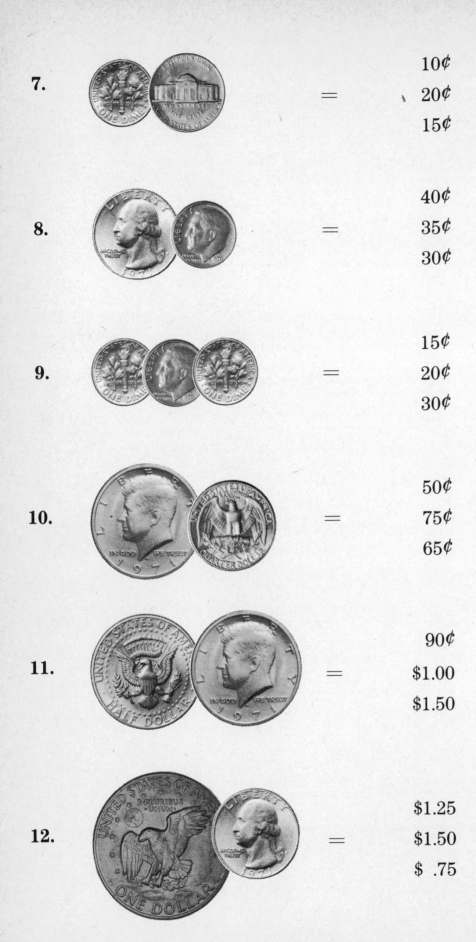

7.   =   10¢
20¢
15¢

8.   =   40¢
35¢
30¢

9.   =   15¢
20¢
30¢

10.   =   50¢
75¢
65¢

11.   =   90¢
$1.00
$1.50

12.   = $1.25
$1.50
$ .75

The Story of Money

Most people in our country use money almost every day. But a long, long time ago, people did not use money at all. There were no coins or paper money. When people wanted to get something, they had to trade something else for it.

This is how trading worked.

Ogg was a farmer. He grew cabbages. He had more than enough cabbages to feed his family of ten. But they all needed shoes. They let Ogg know it, too!

So Ogg went to see Zogg, who made shoes for a living. "I'll trade you 300 cabbages for ten pairs of shoes, Zogg," said Ogg. "My cabbages, you know, are the best in town."

"Your cabbages are beautiful," said Zogg. "But what am I going to do with 300 of them? Besides, I don't even *like* cabbage. If you had a cow, though, we might make a trade."

So Ogg went to see Togg. Togg owned many cows. "Hello there, Togg!" cried Ogg. "Want to trade a cow for 300 cabbages?"

Togg looked surprised. "Are you sick or something, Ogg?" he asked. "What would I do with 300 cabbages? I could use pigs, though. Come back with two pigs, and we might make a trade."

So Ogg visited Yogga, who ran a pig farm. Her pigs were eating her out of house and home. "Am I glad to see you!" cried Yogga when she saw Ogg and his cabbages. "How about trading me those cabbages. I'll give you two pigs for them."

"Sold!" cried Ogg. "There are 300 cabbages here. And I know your pigs will love them."

So Ogg traded his cabbages for two of Yogga's pigs. Then he went back to Togg. He traded the two pigs for one of Togg's cows. And with his new cow, he went off to see Zogg.

Zogg was not in his shop when Ogg got there. Ogg had to wait a long time for him. But at last Zogg showed up. "Nice cow you have there, Ogg," said Zogg. "A present for your wife?"

Ogg was very angry. But he knew he had to be nice to Zogg if he wanted shoes. "No," said Ogg, "this cow is not a present for my wife. You told me this morning you would trade shoes for a cow. I have been trading all day to get this cow! Now I want to trade her to you for ten pairs of shoes."

"Let me think about it for a while," said Zogg. And he thought and thought and thought. Poor Ogg almost fell asleep. But at last Zogg said, "All right. The shoes are yours."

Ogg came home with the shoes for his family. And now everyone was happy. Ogg's family had shoes. Zogg had his cow. Togg had his pigs. And Yogga had cabbages to feed her pigs.

But poor old Ogg was very tired from his day of trading. He went straight to bed and fell asleep. It could be that he had a dream. He might have dreamed of the day when people would start using money. If people used money, Ogg could have sold his cabbages for money. Then he could have used the money to buy his family shoes. He could have saved himself a lot of time. And he could have saved himself a lot of work.

We don't know if Ogg had a dream about money. But one day, two wise people got together. They had a great idea — using money! They brought all the people of their town together. They told the people that their trading days were over. They said they would teach the people how to use *money*.

The two wise people placed six bags of salt on a table. "From now on," they said, "you can give six bags of salt for one cow." Then they took away three of the bags of salt. "For three bags of salt," they said, "you can buy one pig." Then they took away two more bags of salt. "For one bag of salt," they said, "you can buy ten baskets of wheat. Or you can buy one pair of shoes. Or. . . ." And the two wise people went on and on. They named all the things people needed. They named all the things people had been trading.

At first the people just smiled as they listened to the two wise people. But they soon caught on. Salt was something that everyone needed. You could always trade it, so you could always use it to get things you needed. *And it was easy to carry around*.

How happy the people were! At last they had *money*. They would not have to spend all their time trading.

Everyone in the town began using salt as money. After a while, the people in the next town began using salt money, too. Soon people all over the country were using salt money. Then people in the next country found out what was going on. They saw how much better it was to use money than to trade. They started using salt money, too.

And so it went from country to country. Everyone liked using money. But not everyone thought that salt made the best money. In some countries, people thought it was better to use seashells for money. Others used special balls of clay, special stones, or special pieces of wood.

It was many years after this that people began using metals for money. At first, bars of copper, silver, or gold were used. Then the first metal coin was made. Metal was beaten into a round, flat shape. Then a picture was stamped on one of its sides.

China may have been the first place where coins were made. But the first coins we are sure about came from Lydia — 2,600 years ago! Lydia was a country in Asia Minor, where Turkey is today.

Coins were also made in the Greek islands, not far from Lydia. The coins that the Greeks made were very beautiful. They were made of silver. And they had pictures on both sides. Greek coins were used as money in many countries.

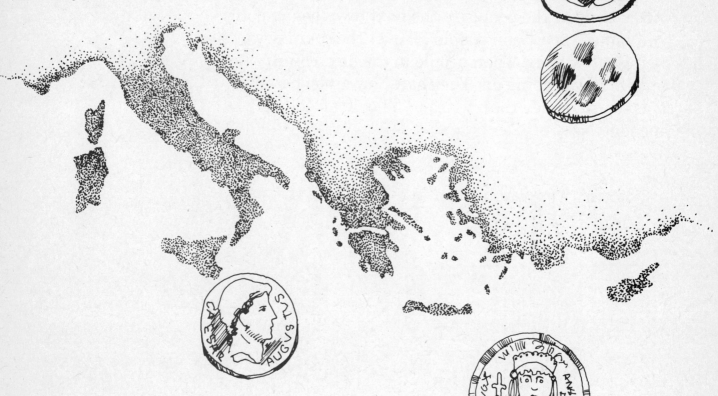

As time went on, more and more countries made their own coins. Coins were made in Africa, Asia, and Europe. But the coins of the Romans became the most important. Roman coins were used for hundreds of years in every part of the Roman Empire. And the Roman Empire covered a good part of the world.

Today, every country has its own coins. Paper money has been in use for only a hundred years or so. But most countries now have their own paper money, too. Making paper money was another step taken so that money would be easier to carry and use.

Coins of the United States

In America's early days, people used English, French, and Spanish coins as money. It was not until 1793 that the first United States coins were made.

English

Spanish

French

Coins were made in a place called a mint. The first United States mint was in Philadelphia. This mint turned out gold coins (eagles), silver coins (dollars), and copper coins (cents). Other coins — half-eagles, half-dollars, and so on — were also made there. The gold eagle was worth the most — ten dollars.

Gold Eagle

Half-Eagle

Silver Dollar

Cent

Today there are three mints that make United States coins. These mints are in Philadelphia, Denver, and San Francisco. All of our money is in dollars and cents now. The metals used in our coins are copper, tin, zinc, and nickel. No gold or silver coins are made anymore.

United States coins have changed in other ways over the years. At one time, we had a picture of an American Indian on the penny. And we once had a nickel with a buffalo pictured on it. "Indian head pennies" and "buffalo nickels" are hard to find today. Not long ago, Benjamin Franklin was pictured on the half-dollar. You can still find some of these coins around.

Today the front sides (heads) of all our coins carry pictures of famous Americans.

Abraham Lincoln is on the penny (one cent).

The back (tail) shows the Lincoln Memorial, a building in Washington, D.C.

Thomas Jefferson is on the nickel (five cents).

The back shows Monticello, Jefferson's home in Virginia.

Franklin D. Roosevelt is on the dime (ten cents).

The back shows the torch of freedom with laurel and oak leaves.

George Washington is on the quarter (twenty-five cents).

The back shows the American bald eagle.

John F. Kennedy is on the half-dollar (fifty cents).

The back shows the seal of our presidents.

Dwight D. Eisenhower is on the dollar (one dollar).

The back shows the American bald eagle landing on the moon.

The penny and the nickel have smooth edges. All of the other coins have rough edges. They have many lines cut into them. Many blind people can tell one coin from another by touch. Can you?

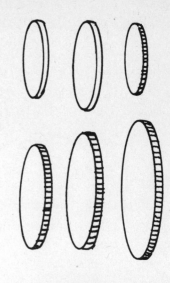

A dollar coin, with Susan B. Anthony on its front, first came out in 1978. Susan B. Anthony helped organize the group that got women the right to vote. Many people collect this coin. Others find they mistake it for a quarter, so they try to avoid using it. For these reasons, you do not see many of these dollars being used today.

A dollar coin with Dwight D. Eisenhower on its front was produced from 1971 to 1978. Eisenhower was the 34th United States president. People collect these coins, too. But you still see them being used from time to time.

George Washington's picture is on the front of the dollar bill (one dollar).

The back shows the Great Seal of the United States.

All of our paper money is printed in black and green. It is bigger in size than the bill shown here. Our laws say that only the government can print pictures of our money in green. And only the government can print pictures of bills that are the same size as the real bills. Can you guess why we have such laws?

Name the Coins

Write the name and value of each coin in the blank next to it.

1.

   quarter   twenty-five cents

2.

3.

4.

5.

6.

7.

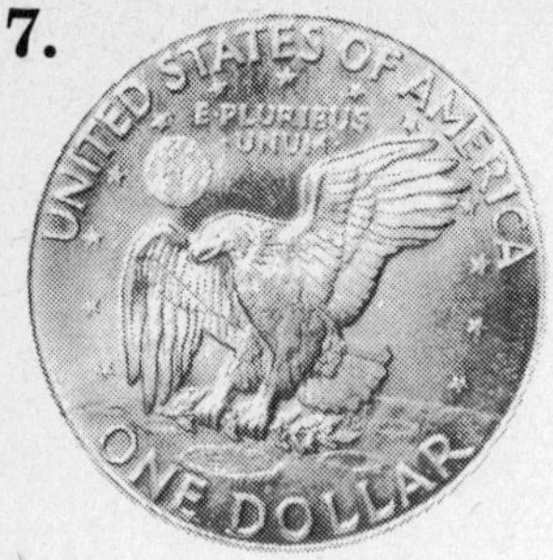
UNITED STATES OF AMERICA
E PLURIBUS UNUM
ONE DOLLAR

8.

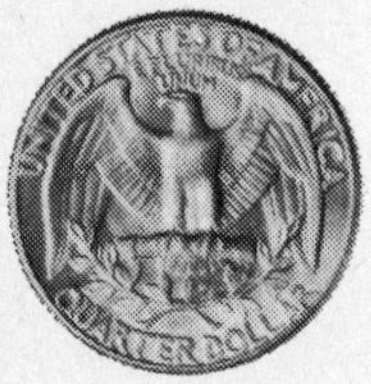
UNITED STATES OF AMERICA
QUARTER DOLLAR

9.

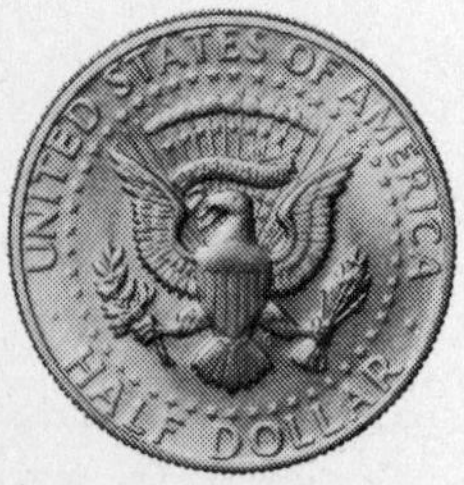
UNITED STATES OF AMERICA
HALF DOLLAR

10.

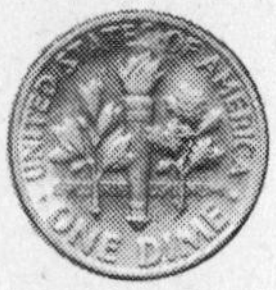
UNITED STATES OF AMERICA
ONE DIME

11.

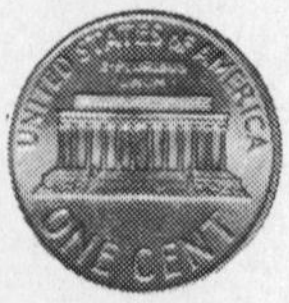
UNITED STATES OF AMERICA
ONE CENT

12.

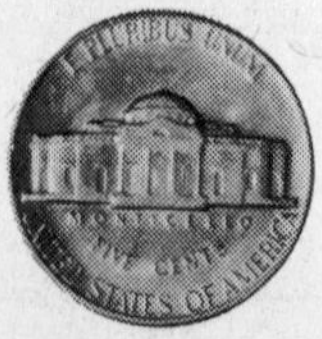
E PLURIBUS UNUM
UNITED STATES OF AMERICA

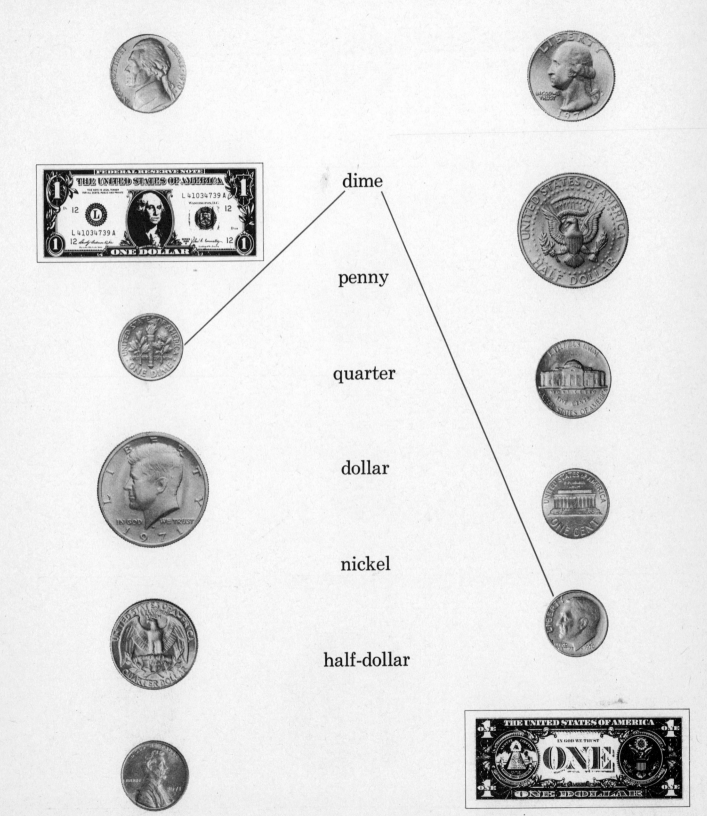

Name the Money

Draw lines from each name to the money it names.
All the money must be named.

dime

penny

quarter

dollar

nickel

half-dollar

Write the name of each coin in the blank below it.

1.

_____ dollar _____

2.

_____

3.

_____

4.

_____

5.

_____

6.

_____

7.

_____

8.

_____

9.

_____

10.

_____

11.

_____

12.

_____

NAME _____

Name the Money

Write the name of each coin or bill in the blank below it.

1.

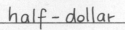 half-dollar _____ _____ _____

2.

_____ _____ _____ _____

3.

_____ _____ _____ _____

4.

_____ _____ _____

5.

_____ _____ _____ _____

6.

_____   _____   _____   _____

7.

_____   _____   _____   _____

8.

_____   _____   _____

9.

_____   _____   _____   _____

10.

_____   _____   _____   _____

Name the Coins and Match the Circles

Draw a line from each coin to its name. Then draw another line from the coin to a circle the same size as the coin. If you cannot tell which circles match which coins, place real coins on the circles.

Names

dime

quarter

penny

half-dollar

dollar

nickel

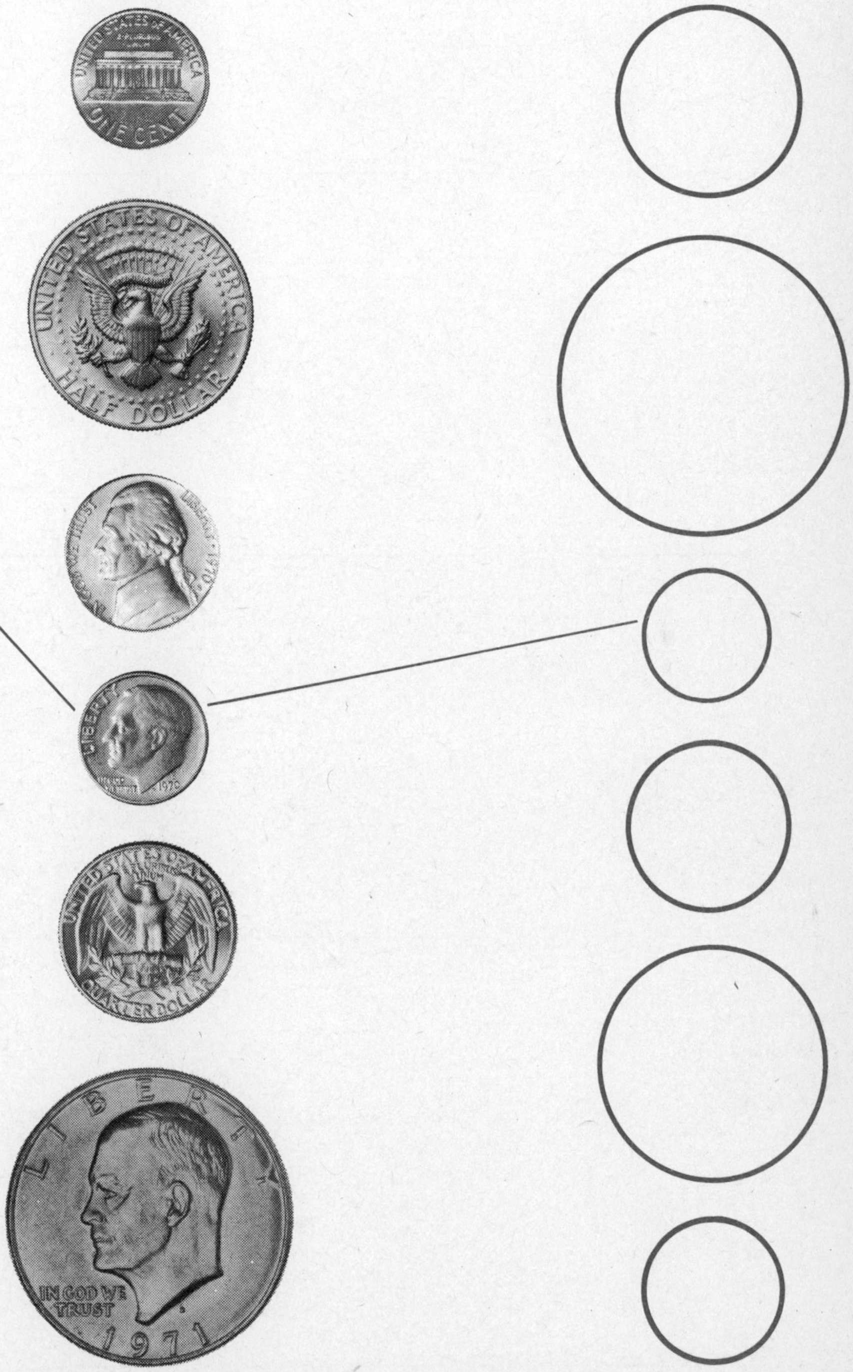

Coins

Circles

Each of these circles is the same size as a United
States coin. Under each circle, write the name of the coin
it matches. Place real coins in the circles if you are not sure.

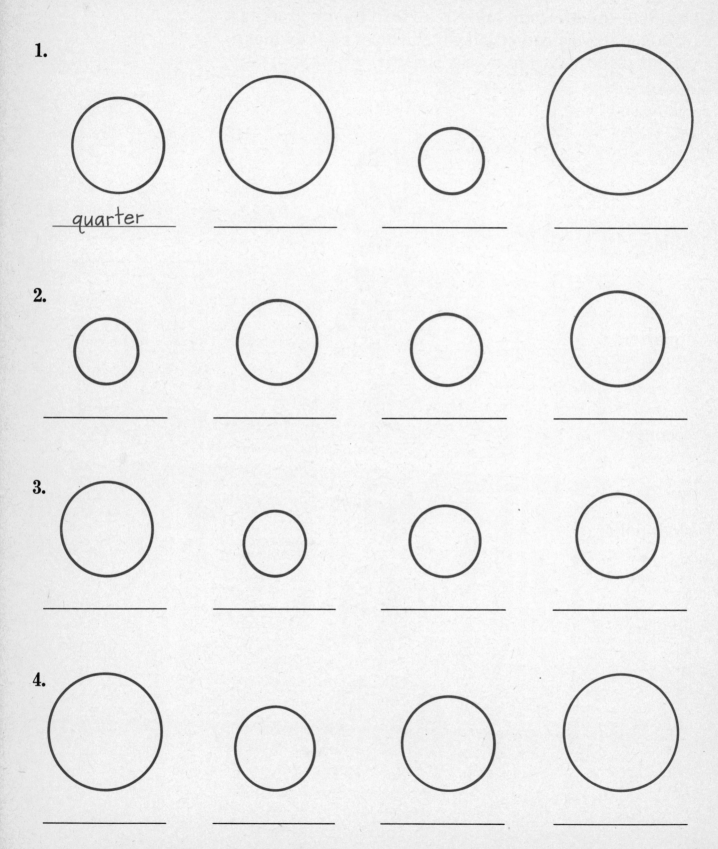

1.

quarter _____ _____ _____

2.

_____ _____ _____ _____

3.

_____ _____ _____ _____

4.

_____ _____ _____ _____

Name the Money

The name of a coin or bill tells you how much it is worth —
its value. The name or value of money can also be written
in numbers. The names or values of United States money
are given here in numbers. In the blank under each
coin or bill, write its value in words.

$ .01 *or* 1¢ $ .05 *or* 5¢ $ .10 *or* 10¢

__one cent__   _____   _____

$ .25 *or* 25¢ $ .50 *or* 50¢ $1.00 *or* $1

_____   _____

_____

$1.00 *or* $1

_____

When numbers are used to name money, signs are
used with them. The sign for dollars is $. The sign for
cents is ¢. *But these two signs are never used at the same
time.* When the dollar sign is used, the decimal point
is placed before the numbers for cents.

In the blank under each coin or bill, write its value in numbers. Use the dollar sign and a decimal point.

1.

$ .25 _____   _____   _____   _____   _____

2.

_____   _____   _____   _____   _____

3.

_____   _____   _____   _____

4.

_____   _____   _____   _____   _____

Name the Money

In the blank under each coin or bill, write its value in numbers. Use the cents sign for amounts under a dollar. Use the dollar sign for amounts equal to a dollar.

1.

10¢ _____   _____   _____   _____   _____

2.

_____   _____   _____   _____   _____

3.

_____   _____   _____   _____   _____

4.

_____   _____   _____   _____

Draw a line from each name or value to the coin it names.

nickel

$ .50

10¢

twenty-five cents

penny

$1.00

$ .01

fifty cents

$ .05

dollar

5¢

50¢

dime

$ .25

$ .10

$1

quarter

half-dollar

1¢

one cent

ten cents

25¢

five cents

one dollar

Counting Money

You will often have more than one coin. Then you will want to know how much money you have altogether. To find out, you add up the value of the coins. This is called *counting money*.

5	five
1	six
1	seven
+1	eight
8	**The sum is eight.**

Counting money is the same as adding numbers. The total value you get is called the *sum*.

5¢   +   1¢   +   1¢   +   1¢   =   8¢

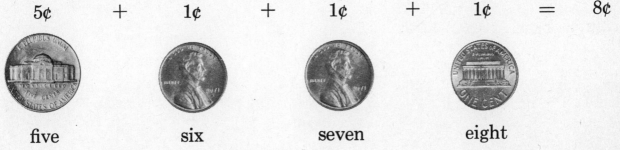

five   six   seven   eight

The sum is eight cents.

Here are some more examples. Say the words as you count from left to right. Coins of higher value are counted first.

five   six   seven   eight   nine   ten

The sum is ten cents.

ten   fifteen   sixteen   seventeen   eighteen

The sum is eighteen cents.

How Much Is It?

Count each of these groups of coins from left to right.
As you count, say the words and write them in the blanks
under the coins. Then write the sum in words.

1.

one   _two_   _three_   _four_   _five_

The sum is _____ _five cents_ _____

2.

_____ _____ _____ _____ _____ _____ _____

The sum is _____

3.

_____ _____ _____

The sum is _____

4.

_____ _____ _____ _____

The sum is _____

5.

_____ _____ _____

The sum is _____

6.

_____ _____ _____ _____

The sum is _____

How Much Is It?

Count each of these groups of coins from left to right.
As you count, say the words and write them in the blanks.
Write the sum in words under the last coin.

1.

ten   eleven   twelve   thirteen   fourteen cents

2.

____ ____ ____ ____ ____

3.

____ ____ ____ ____ ____

4.

____ ____ ____ ____ ____

5.

____ ____ ____ ____ ____

6.

____ ____ ____ ____ ____

7.

_____ _____ _____ _____ _____

8.

_____ _____ _____ _____ _____

9.

_____ _____ _____ _____ _____

10.

_____ _____ _____ _____ _____

11.

_____ _____ _____ _____ _____

12.

_____ _____ _____ _____ _____

How Much Is It?

Count each group of coins from left to right. As you count, say the words, *but write the amounts in numbers.* Write the sum, using the cents sign, under the last coin in each group.

1.

   _____10_____ _____15 ¢_____

2.

   _____ _____ _____ _____

3.

   _____ _____ _____

4.

   _____ _____ _____ _____ _____

5.

   _____ _____ _____ _____ _____

6.

   _____ _____ _____ _____ _____

7.

_____ _____ _____ _____

8.

_____ _____ _____ _____ _____

9.

_____ _____ _____ _____ _____

10.

_____ _____ _____ _____ _____

11.

_____ _____ _____ _____ _____ _____

12.

_____ _____ _____ _____ _____ _____

How Much Is It?

Count each group of coins from left to right. As you count, say the words. Then write the amounts in numbers. Write the sum, using the cents sign, under the last coin in each group.

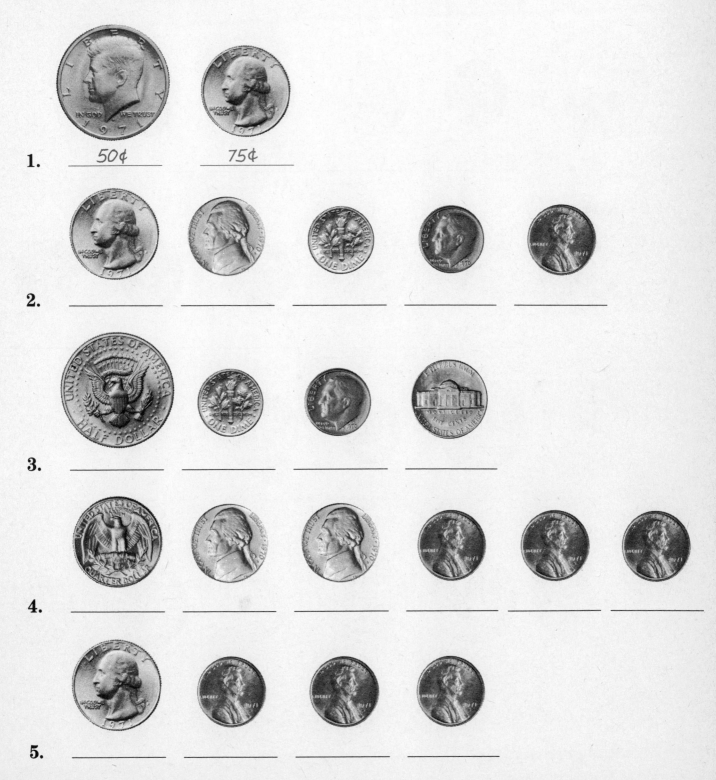

1. _____50¢_____   _____75¢_____

2. _____ _____ _____ _____ _____

3. _____ _____ _____ _____

4. _____ _____ _____ _____ _____ _____

5. _____ _____ _____ _____

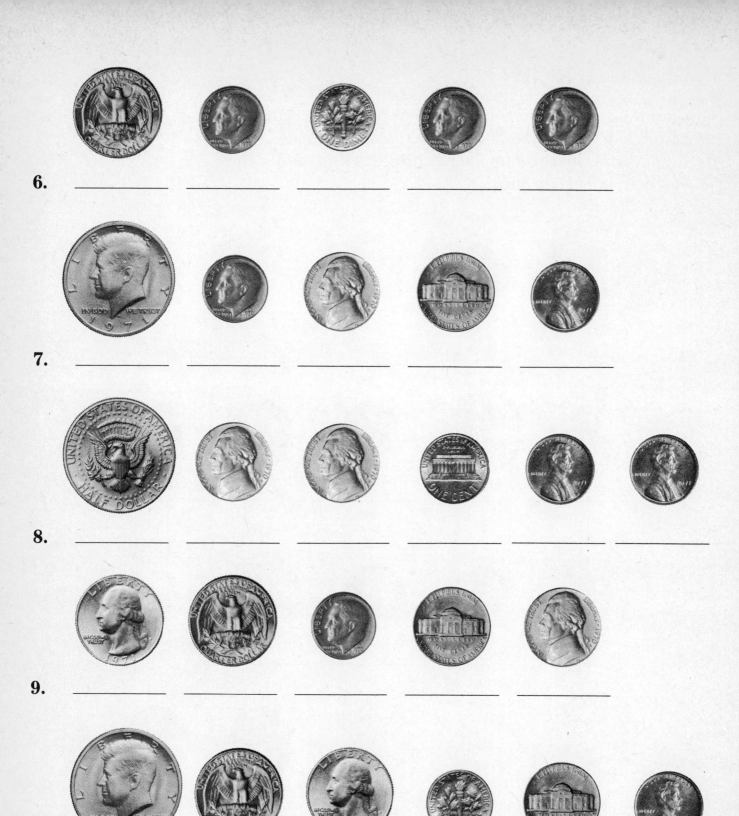

6. _____ _____ _____ _____ _____

7. _____ _____ _____ _____ _____

8. _____ _____ _____ _____ _____ _____

9. _____ _____ _____ _____ _____

10. _____ _____ _____ _____ _____ _____

How Much Is It?

When coins are counted, their sum can be written in three ways. Count each of these groups of coins and write each sum three different ways.

1.　　　　4 pennies

$.04　　　4¢　　　　four cents

2.　　　　2 nickels

_____　_____　_____

3.　　　　2 dimes

_____　_____　_____

4.　　　　2 quarters

_____　_____　_____

5.　　　　2 pennies

_____　_____　_____

6.　　　　3 dimes

_____　_____　_____

7.　　　　3 pennies

_____　_____　_____

8.　　　　3 nickels

_____　_____　_____

9. 4 dimes

10. 3 quarters

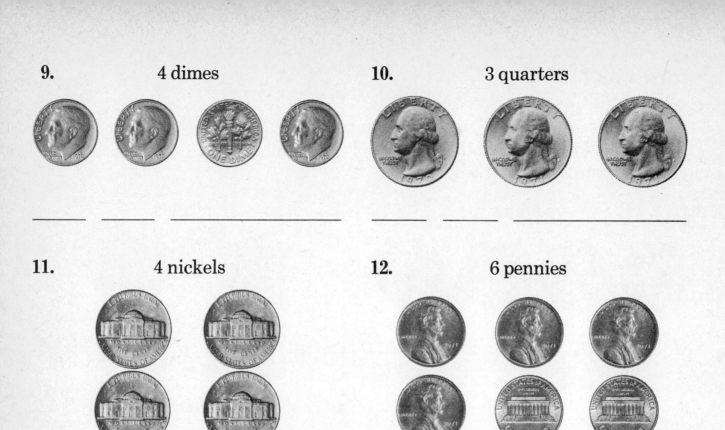

_____   _____

11. 4 nickels

12. 6 pennies

_____   _____

13. 6 nickels

14. 10 dimes

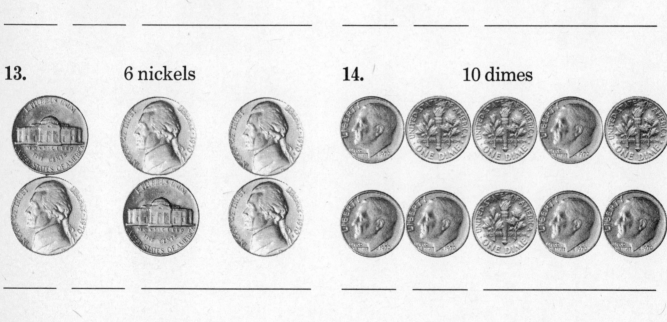

_____   _____

15. 5 dimes

16. 2 half-dollars

_____   _____

How Much Is It?

Count each group of coins. Write each sum in three different ways.

1.

$ .10   10¢   <u>ten cents</u>   _____ _____ _____

3.

_____ _____ _____

4.

_____ _____ _____

5.

_____ _____ _____

6.

_____ _____ _____

7.

_____ _____ _____

8.

_____ _____ _____

Count each group of coins. Write each sum using the
cents sign.

9.

_____10¢_____

10.

_____

11.

_____

12.

_____

13.

_____

14.

_____

15.

_____

Coin Addition Table

Fill in the empty squares by adding the coins in the
left-hand column to the coins in the top row.

+	(penny)	(nickel)	(dime)	(quarter)	(half dollar)
(penny)	2¢				
(nickel)					
(dime)		15¢			
(quarter)					
(half dollar)					

Money Addition Table

Fill in the empty squares by adding the money in the
left-hand column to the money in the top row.

+	1¢	2¢	3¢	4¢	5¢	6¢	7¢	8¢	9¢	10¢
1¢										
2¢										
3¢				7¢						
4¢										
5¢								13¢		
6¢										
7¢										
8¢										
9¢										
10¢										

How Much Is It?

Find the value of each group of coins. Write each sum using the dollar sign and a decimal point.

1.

$.06

2.

_____

3.

_____

4.

_____

5.

_____

6.

_____

7.

_____

8.

_____

9.

_____

10.

_____

11.

_____

12.

_____

13.

_____

14.

_____

15.

_____

16.

_____

How Much Is It?

How many of each coin are shown? How much are they worth? Write your answers in the blanks under the coins.

1.

<u>ten pennies</u>　　<u>10¢</u>

2.

_____   _____

3.

_____   _____

4.

_____   _____

5.

_____   _____

6.

_____   _____

7.

_____   _____

8.

9.

_____ _____   _____ _____

10. 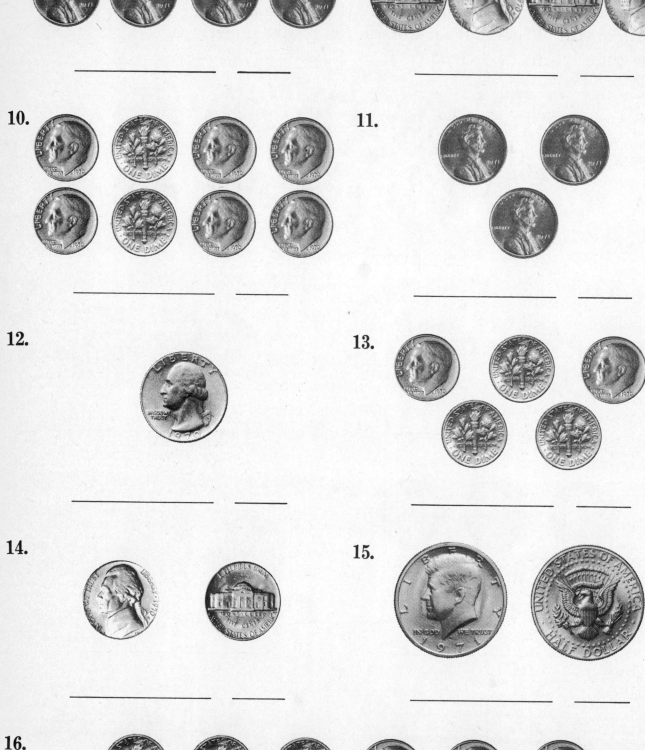   **11.**

_____   _____ _____

12.   **13.**

_____   _____

14.   **15.**

_____   _____

16.

_____ _____

NAME _____

Name the Coins

Sometimes one coin has the same value as two or
more other coins. In these exercises, the coins on the
right are worth the same amount of money as the coins
on the left. Write the names of the coins on the right
in the blanks.

1.   **are worth 1**

5 pennies   *nickel*

2.   **are worth 1**

2 nickels   _____

3.   **are worth 1**

2 dimes and 1 nickel   _____

4.     **are worth 1**

2 quarters   _____

5.    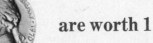   **are worth 1**

1 quarter, 1 dime , and 3 nickels   _____

6.

 **are worth 1**

3 dimes and 4 nickels

_____

7.

   **are worth 1**

5 dimes

_____

8.

   **are worth 1**

1 half-dollar and 2 quarters

_____

9.

 **are worth 1**

4 quarters

_____

10.

  **are worth 1**

2 half-dollars

_____

Adding Money

A dollar bill is worth the same as the Eisenhower dollar.
Make X's on the blanks under the coins that add up to
one dollar.

1  **is worth:**

1.

   X   X   X

2.

3.

4.

Make X's on the blanks under the coins that add up to the coin on the right.

5.    are worth 1

     X   _____   _____   _____   X

6.     are worth 1

_____

7.       are worth 1

_____

8.      are worth 1

_____

9.    are worth 1

_____

Which Coin Is It?

When the coins on the left are counted, they will equal a single coin. Write the name of the coin in the blank on the right.

1.

_____dime_____

2.

_____

3.

_____

4.

_____

5.

_____

6.

_____

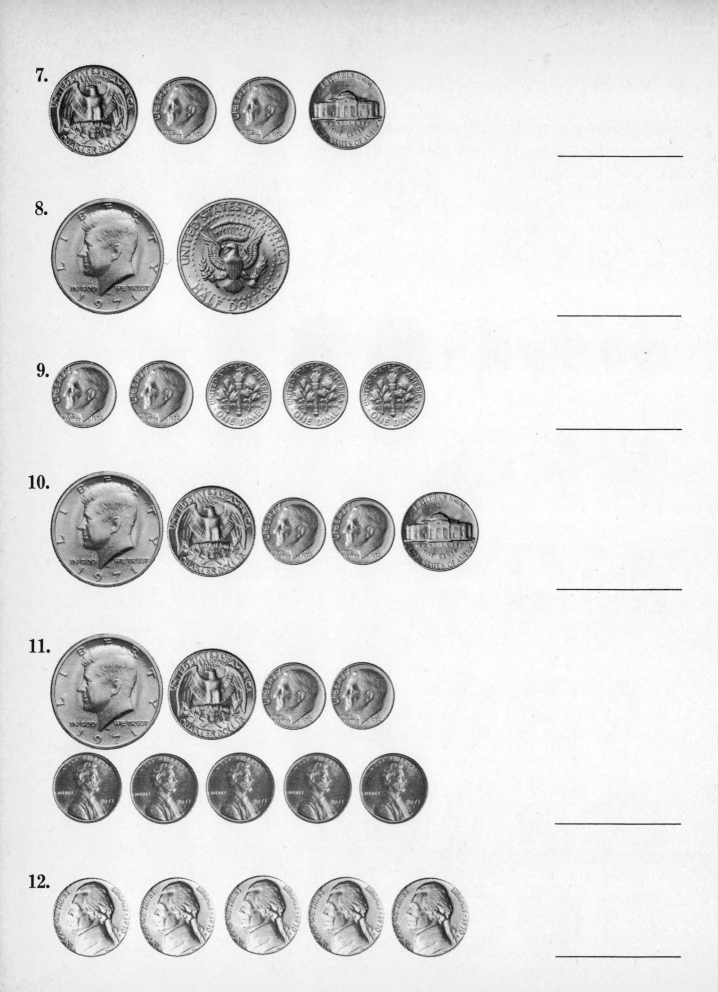

7. _____

8. _____

9. _____

10. _____

11. _____

12. _____

Matching Money

Make X's in the blanks under the amounts of money that match in each row.

1. three cents $1.00   one dollar   50¢

     ____   X   ____   X   ____   ____

2. 75¢   fifty cents   43¢   50¢   penny   half-dollar

     ____   ____   ____   ____   ____   ____

3.   nickel   forty cents $ .50   37¢   5¢

     ____   ____   ____   ____   ____

4. 30¢   25¢   nineteen cents   quarter   forty-two cents $ .05

     ____   ____   ____   ____   ____   ____

5. 13¢   dime $ .25   11¢   quarter   cent

     ____   ____   ____   ____   ____   ____

6. 19¢   penny   seventy-five cents   cent $ .01

     ____   ____   ____   ____   ____

7. quarter   37¢   16¢ $ .30   thirty-seven cents

     ____   ____   ____   ____   ____

8.    14¢   25¢   twenty-five cents $ .05   quarter

____   ___ ___   ___   ___

9. nickel   11¢   eleven cents $ .19   dime

___   ___   ___   ___   ___

10. $ .25      56¢   fifty cents   nickel $1

___   ___   ___   ___   ___

11. dime   13¢ $ .05   23¢   nickel   quarter

___   ___   ___   ___   ___

12. 64¢   sixty-four cents   nickel $ .10

___   ___   ___   ___

13. one dollar   50¢ $1.00 $ .01 $1

___   ___   ___   ___

14. 10¢   twelve cents    $ .15   dime   13¢   penny

___   ___   ___   ___

Matching Money

Make X's in the blanks under the amounts of money
that match in each row.

1.  half-dollar   20¢   quarter $.30   twenty-five cents

    X   ____   X   ____   X

2. quarter $.37   87¢   thirty-seven cents $.56

  ____   ____   ____   ____   ____   ____

3. $.10   one dollar   50¢   ninety cents   100¢   46¢ $1.00

  ____   ____   ____   ____   ____   ____   ____

4.  34¢   seventeen cents $.60   quarter   35¢

  ____   ____   ____   ____   ____

5. dime $.64   75¢   eighty-three cents $.14   83¢

  ____   ____   ____   ____   ____   ____

6. $.80   sixty cents $.50   quarter      49¢   half dollar

  ____   ____   ____   ____   ____   ____

7. twenty cents $.25   20¢   30¢   fifteen cents

  ____   ____   ____   ____   ____

8. 75¢ nickel $.70  seventy-five cents 15¢

___ ___ ___ ___ ___

9. dime  sixteen cents  75¢ 70¢

___ ___ ___ ___ ___

10. $.18 twenty-five cents $.78 18¢ 92¢ eighteen cents

___ ___ ___ ___

11. ninety-one cents    25¢ $.31 36¢

___ ___ ___ ___

12. 88¢ $1.00 fifty cents $.25 one dollar 75¢ $.10

___ ___ ___ ___ ___

13. nickel cent $.45 55¢  forty-five cents

___ ___ ___ ___ ___

14.  $.17 seven cents  12¢

___ ___ ___ ___

Sum Circles!

Find the value of each group of coins on the left. Write the sum in the blank on the right, using numbers and the cents sign. Then, in the space over your answer, draw a circle the same size as the coin that is the sum. Use a coin for tracing if you want to.

1.   =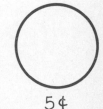

                                                      5¢

2.   =

                                                      _____

3.  =

                                                      _____

4.   =

                                                      _____

5.   =

                                                      _____

6. 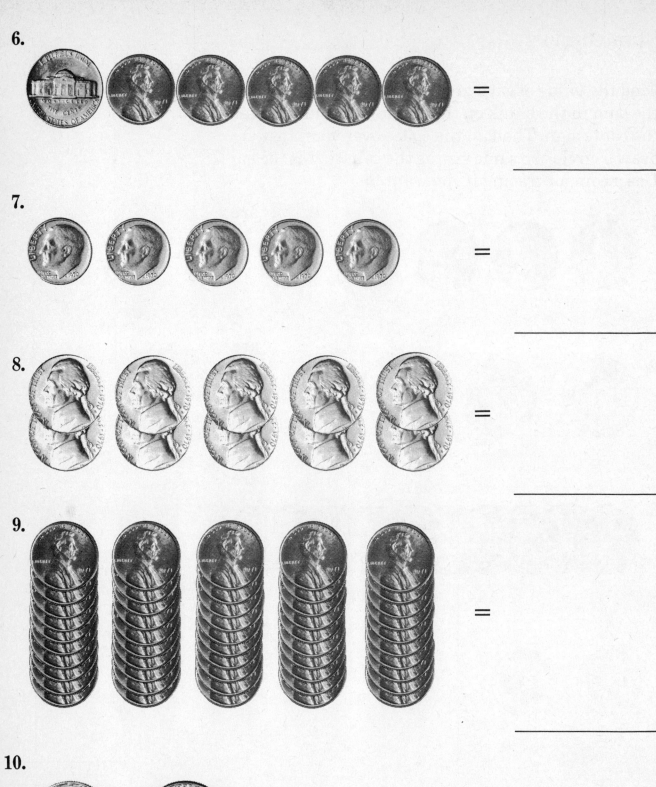 = _____

7. = _____

8. = _____

9. = _____

10.  = _____

What Are They Worth?

Write the total value of the coins in the blanks. Use numbers and the cents sign.

1.

are worth

10 ¢

2.

are worth

_____

3.

are worth

_____

4.

are worth

_____

5.

are worth

_____

6.

are worth

_____

7.

       are worth

_____

8.

     are worth

_____

9.

       are worth

_____

10.

      are worth

_____

11.

    are worth

_____

12.

      are worth

_____

How Much Is It?

Write the total value of the coins in three different ways.

1.

$.75   75¢   seventy-five cents

2.

_____ _____ _____

3.

_____ _____ _____

4.

_____ _____ _____

5.

_____ _____ _____

6.

_____ _____ _____

7.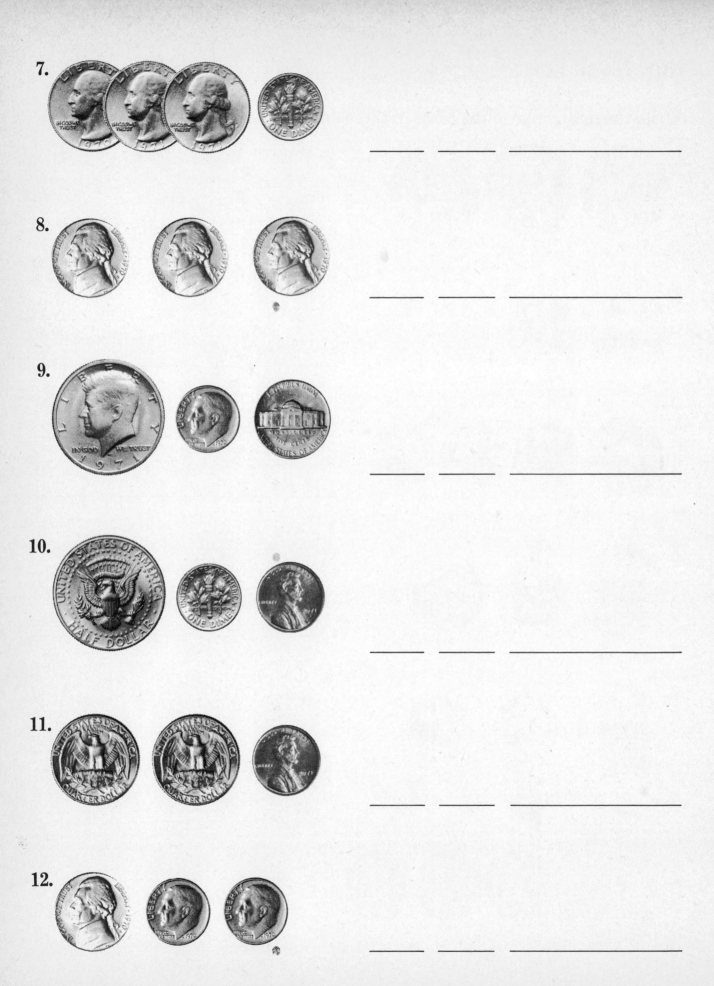

_____ _____ _____

8.

_____ _____ _____

9.

_____ _____ _____

10.

_____ _____ _____

11.

_____ _____ _____

12.

_____ _____ _____

Matching Money

Draw lines between the amounts that are the same.

1. thirty cents ——————————— 25¢ ——————— $ .41
   forty-one cents ————————— 30¢ ——————— $ .25
   twenty-five cents ———————— 41¢ ——————— $ .30

2. twenty-one cents   15¢ $ .21
   fifteen cents   21¢ $ .27
   twenty-seven cents   27¢ $ .15

3. forty-five cents   60¢ $ .30
   sixty cents   52¢ $ .52
   fifty-two cents   30¢ $ .45
   thirty cents   45¢ $ .60

4. ninety cents   24¢ $ .90
   fourteen cents   90¢ $ .24
   twenty-four cents   14¢ $ .17
   seventeen cents   17¢ $ .14

5. fifteen cents   71¢ $ .15
   ninety-eight cents   11¢ $ .98
   eleven cents   98¢ $ .11
   seventy-one cents   15¢ $ .71

6. thirty-four cents   34¢ $ .65
   eighty-two cents   82¢ $ .19
   sixty-five cents   19¢ $ .82
   nineteen cents   65¢ $ .34

7.	seven cents	6¢	$ .11
	six cents	11¢	$ .06
	eleven cents	13¢	$ .07
	thirteen cents	7¢	$ .13
8.	twenty-one cents	51¢	$ .15
	fifteen cents	21¢	$ .27
	twenty-seven cents	27¢	$ .51
	fifty-one cents	15¢	$ .21
9.	fifteen cents	40¢	$ .15
	thirty cents	60¢	$ .30
	forty cents	30¢	$ .40
	sixty cents	15¢	$ .60
10.	seventeen cents	15¢	$ .17
	eleven cents	98¢	$ .11
	ninety-eight cents	11¢	$ .98
	fifteen cents	17¢	$ .15
11.	nineteen cents	65¢	$ .34
	sixty-five cents	19¢	$ .82
	eighty-two cents	82¢	$ .19
	thirty-four cents	34¢	$ .65
12.	twenty-seven cents	27¢	$ .21
	fifteen cents	31¢	$ .27
	twenty-one cents	15¢	$ .31
	thirty-one cents	21¢	$ .15

How Much Is It?

Find the sum of each group of coins.

You read: 1 dime,   1 nickel,   and   3 pennies

You think:

You count: 10   15   16   17   18¢

1. 1 dime, 1 nickel, and 2 pennies = 17 ¢
2. 1 dime, 1 nickel, and 1 penny = ___ ¢
3. 1 dime, 1 nickel, and 6 pennies = ___ ¢
4. 1 dime and 3 pennies = ___ ¢
5. 2 dimes and 1 penny = ___ ¢
6. 2 nickels and 3 pennies = ___ ¢
7. 1 dime and 3 nickels = ___ ¢
8. 1 nickel and 4 pennies = ___ ¢
9. 2 dimes and 2 pennies = ___ ¢
10. 1 dime, 1 nickel, and 4 pennies = ___ ¢
11. 1 dime, 2 nickels, and 2 pennies = ___ ¢
12. 1 dime and 4 pennies = ___ ¢
13. 1 dime and 7 pennies = ___ ¢
14. 3 nickels and 3 pennies = ___ ¢
15. 1 dime, 1 nickel, and 8 pennies = ___ ¢

Find the sum of each group of coins.

You read: 1 dime,   2 nickels,   and   10 pennies

You think:

You count: 10   20 $ .30

16. 1 dime, 2 nickels, and 3 pennies   = $___.23___

17. 4 nickels and 1 penny   = $__._____

18. 2 dimes and 3 pennies   = $__._____

19. 1 dime, 1 nickel, and 6 pennies   = $__._____

20. 1 dime and 9 pennies   = $__._____

21. 23 pennies   = $__._____

22. 2 dimes and 2 pennies   = $__._____

23. 4 nickels   = $__._____

24. 1 dime, 1 nickel, and 9 pennies   = $__._____

25. 1 dime and 2 nickels   = $__._____

26. 2 dimes   = $__._____

27. 1 dime and 13 pennies   = $__._____

28. 3 dimes, 2 nickels, and 4 pennies   = $__._____

29. 3 nickels and 12 pennies   = $__._____

30. 5 dimes and 5 nickels   = $__._____

How Much Is It?

Find the sum of each group of coins.

You read: 1 quarter,   2 dimes,   2 nickels,   and   1 penny

You think:

You count: 25   45   55   56¢

1. 1 quarter, 2 dimes, and 1 penny   =   46 ¢

2. 1 quarter, 1 dime, 1 nickel, and 3 pennies   =   ____¢

3. 1 quarter and 3 pennies   =   ____¢

4. 1 quarter, 1 nickel, and 1 penny   =   ____¢

5. 1 quarter, 1 dime, 1 nickel, and 1 penny   =   ____¢

6. 1 quarter, 2 dimes, and 4 pennies   =   ____¢

7. 1 quarter and 1 penny   =   ____¢

8. 1 quarter and 1 nickel   =   ____¢

9. 1 quarter and 1 dime   =   ____¢

10. 3 quarters and 2 nickels   =   ____¢

11. 2 quarters, 3 dimes, and 2 nickels   =   ____¢

12. 1 quarter, 4 dimes, and 2 nickels   =   ____¢

13. 3 quarters and 17 pennies   =   ____¢

14. 2 quarters and six nickels   =   ____¢

15. 1 quarter, 4 nickels, and 29 pennies   =   ____¢

Find the sum of each group of coins.

You read:	1 half-dollar,	1 quarter,	1 dime,	1 nickel, and 1 penny

You think:

You count:	50	75	85	90	$ .91

16. 1 half-dollar, 1 quarter, 2 dimes, and 3 pennies   = $ .98

17. 1 half-dollar, 2 dimes, and 3 pennies   = $._____

18. 1 half-dollar, 1 nickel, and 2 pennies   = $._____

19. 1 quarter, 4 dimes, and 2 pennies   = $._____

20. 1 half-dollar and 25 pennies   = $._____

21. 1 half-dollar, 1 quarter, 1 dime, and 3 pennies   = $._____

22. 1 half-dollar, 1 nickel, and 1 penny   = $._____

23. 1 half-dollar, 1 quarter, 1 dime, and 2 nickels   = $._____

24. 3 quarters and 3 nickels   = $._____

25. 1 half-dollar, 1 quarter, 2 dimes, and 2 pennies   = $._____

26. 1 half-dollar, 1 nickel, and 4 pennies   = $._____

27. 1 half-dollar, 3 nickels, and 2 pennies   = $._____

28. 1 half-dollar, 3 dimes, and 2 nickels   = $._____

29. 1 half-dollar, 4 dimes, and 4 pennies   = $._____

30. 1 half-dollar and 2 quarters   = $._____

Counting Money

Whenever you add money and use decimal points, you must line up the decimal points. All the money to the left of a decimal point is dollars. The money to the right of a decimal point is cents. Every 100 cents makes one dollar. There must always be two numbers on the cents side of a decimal point.

```
$1.00        $1.00
  .25         1.00
  .10          .50
-----        -----
$1.35        $2.50
```

$1.00 + $.25 + $.10 = $1.35

one dollar   one dollar and   one dollar and
                    twenty-five cents   thirty-five cents

Here are some more examples. Say the words as you count from left to right. Coins and bills of higher value are counted first.

$1.00 + $1.00 + $.50 = $2.50

one dollar   two dollars   two dollars and fifty cents

$.50 + $.50 + $.05 = $1.05

fifty cents   one dollar   one dollar and five cents

Count each of these groups of coins and bills from left to
right. As you count, say the words. Then write the sum in
the blanks, using the dollar sign and a decimal point.

1. = $ 1.11

2. = $___.___

3. = $___.___

4. = $___.___

5. = $___.___

6. = $___.___

What Are They Worth?

Write in the blanks the total value of the money in each
row on the left. Use the dollar sign and a decimal point.

1.    **are worth** $2.05

2.    **are worth** _____

3.      **are worth** _____

4.    **are worth** _____

5.      **are worth** _____

6.      **are worth** _____

7.

are worth _____

8.

are worth _____

9.

are worth _____

10.

are worth _____

11.

are worth _____

12.

are worth _____

How Much Is It?

Write in the blanks the total value of the money on the left. Use the dollar sign and a decimal point.

1.   $1.27

2.     _____

3.     _____

4.    _____

5.     _____

6.

_____

7.

_____

8.

_____

9.

_____

10.

_____

How Much Is It?

In these exercises, the money has already been counted.
If the sum given is correct, write *Yes* in the blank on
the right. If the sum is not correct, write *No* in the blank.

1. 5 nickels equal a quarter.   _Yes_

2. 4 nickels and 4 pennies = 1 quarter.   _____

3. Three dimes and 25¢ equal a half-dollar.   _____

4. 6 nickels and $ .40 equal 75¢.   _____

5. One half-dollar and five dimes = $1.   _____

6. Five dimes and 2 quarters equal one dollar.   _____

7. 5 pennies and $ .20 equal thirty cents.   _____

8. Six dimes, 3 nickels, and 25¢ = $1.00.   _____

9. 5 half-dollars, $ .25, and five dimes = $1.75.   _____

10. One quarter and 5 dimes equal 75¢.   _____

11. Two dimes, 3 nickels, and 25¢ = sixty cents.   _____

12. Three nickels and 4 dimes equal fifty cents.   _____

13. One half-dollar and $1.25 = $2.75.   _____

14. 2 quarters and ten dimes equal $1.50.   _____

15. $ .09, 4 dimes, 25¢, and a nickel = 89¢.   _____

16. Two dollars, a dime, and 5¢ = $2.15.   _____

17. $1.00 and 3 half-dollars = $4.   _____

18. One dollar, 3 nickels, and $.08 equal $1.23.   _____

19. $3.00, 8 dimes, and a nickel = $3.95.   _____

20. 7 quarters, 25¢, and a penny = two dollars and one cent.   _____

The Money Wheel

Add the coins connected by lines. Write the sums in
the circles. Then add the sums connected by lines until
you get the total value of the money wheel.

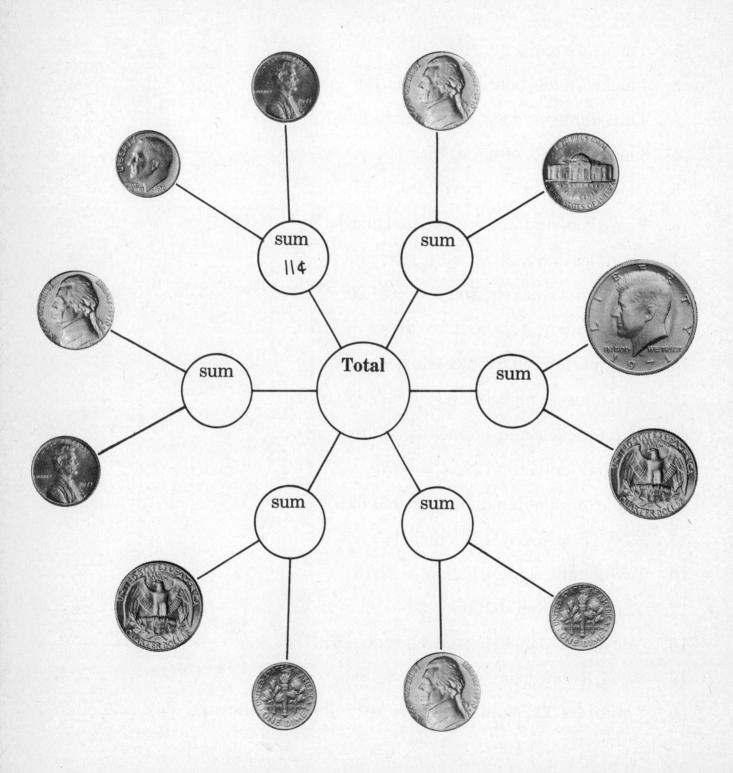

How Much Is It?

Find the sum of each group of money.

You read: 1 dollar,   1 dime,   1 nickel,   and 2 pennies

You think:

You count: $1 $1.10 $1.15 $1.17

1. 1 dollar, 1 quarter, and 2 dimes   = $ 1.45

2. 2 dollars, 2 quarters, 1 nickel, and 3 pennies   = $___.___

3. 1 dollar, 3 nickels, and 2 pennies   = $___.___

4. 1 dollar, 1 half-dollar, 1 quarter, and 1 penny   = $___.___

5. 3 dollars, 3 dimes, and 1 penny   = $___.___

6. 2 dollars, 3 quarters, and 3 nickels   = $___.___

7. 4 quarters, 2 dimes, 2 nickels, and 3 pennies   = $___.___

8. 1 dollar, 4 dimes, and 3 nickels   = $___.___

9. 4 dollars, 5 dimes, and 5 pennies   = $___.___

10. 1 dollar, 2 quarters, 3 dimes, and 4 pennies   = $___.___

11. 1 dollar, 1 dime, 3 nickels, and 1 penny   = $___.___

12. 2 dollars, 1 half-dollar, and 4 nickels   = $___.___

13. 3 dollars, 1 quarter, and 4 dimes   = $___.___

14. 1 dollar, 2 dimes, 4 nickels, and 8 pennies   = $___.___

15. 4 dollars, 1 quarter, 3 dimes, 1 nickel, and 1 penny   = $___.___

Find the sum of each group of money.

You read: 1 dollar, 2 half-dollars, and 1 dime

You think:

You count: $1 $2 $2.10

16. 1 dollar, 2 half-dollars, and 1 quarter = $ 2.25

17. 2 dollars, 3 quarters, 1 nickel, and 2 pennies = $.

18. 1 dollar, 4 quarters, 2 dimes, and 5 pennies = $.

19. 1 dollar, 1 half-dollar, and 3 nickels = $.

20. 3 dollars, 2 quarters, 1 dime, and 2 nickels = $.

21. 2 dollars, 6 dimes, and 4 pennies = $.

22. 2 dollars, 5 nickels, and 7 pennies = $.

23. 4 dollars, 4 dimes, and 4 pennies = $.

24. 1 dollar, 1 dime, 3 nickels, and 3 pennies = $.

25. 2 dollars, 2 quarters, 2 dimes, and 5 pennies = $.

26. 1 dollar, 2 half-dollars, 1 quarter, and 1 dime = $.

27. 3 dollars, 4 dimes, 5 nickels, and 1 penny = $.

28. 3 half-dollars, 1 nickel, and 2 pennies = $.

29. 2 dollars, 5 nickels, and 3 pennies = $.

30. 5 quarters, 2 dimes, and 1 nickel = $.

NAME _____

How Many Are There?

Fill in the blanks on the right with the number of coins
needed to make the amount on the left.

1. 1 dime   = __10__ pennies

2. 1 nickel   = _____ pennies

3. 12¢   = _____ dime and _____ pennies

4. 1 dime   = _____ nickels

5. 7¢   = _____ nickel and _____ pennies

6. 18¢   = _____ dime, _____ nickel, and _____ pennies

7. 26¢   = _____ dimes, _____ nickel, and _____ penny

8. 19¢   = _____ dime, _____ nickel, and _____ pennies

9. 25¢   = _____ dimes and _____ nickel

10. 1 quarter   = _____ dime, _____ nickel, and _____ pennies

11. 35¢   = _____ quarter and _____ dime

12. 43¢   = _____ quarter, _____ dime, _____ nickel, and _____ pennies

13. 50¢   = _____ half-dollar

14. 1 half-dollar = _____ pennies

15. 50¢   = _____ nickels

16. 1 half-dollar = _____ quarters

17. 60¢   = _____ half-dollar and _____ dime

18. 66¢   = _____ half-dollar, _____ dime, _____ nickel, and _____ penny

19. 73¢   = _____ half-dollar, _____ dimes, and _____ pennies

20. 65¢   = _____ quarters and _____ nickels

Fill in the blanks on the right with the number of coins
or bills needed to make the amount on the left.

21. 75¢   = __3__ quarters

22. 85¢   = _____ half-dollar, _____ quarter, and _____ nickels

23. 95¢   = _____ half-dollar, _____ quarter, and _____ dimes

24. one dollar   = _____ pennies

25. $1.00   = _____ nickels

26. one dollar   = _____ dimes

27. $1   = _____ quarters, _____ dimes, and _____ nickel

28. $1.08   = _____ dollar, _____ nickel, and _____ pennies

29. $1.25   = _____ quarters

30. $1.42   = _____ dollar, _____ dimes, and _____ pennies

31. $1.55   = _____ half-dollars and _____ nickel

32. $1.63   = _____ quarters, _____ dime, and _____ pennies

33. $1.80   = _____ dimes

34. $1.95   = _____ dollar, _____ quarters, and _____ nickels

35. two dollars = _____ pennies

36. $2   = _____ half-dollars

37. $2.45   = _____ dollars, _____ quarter, and _____ dimes

38. $2.84   = _____ dollars, _____ nickels, and _____ pennies

39. $3.07   = _____ dollars, _____ nickel, and _____ pennies

40. $3.90   = _____ dollars, _____ quarters, and _____ pennies

41. $4.55   = _____ dollars, _____ half-dollar, and _____ nickel

42. five dollars = _____ half-dollars

Money Paths

Follow the arrows on each path. Add the coins as you
go. Write the sum on each line. Then write the total sum
of all the coins at the bottom of the page.

Path 1   **Path 2**

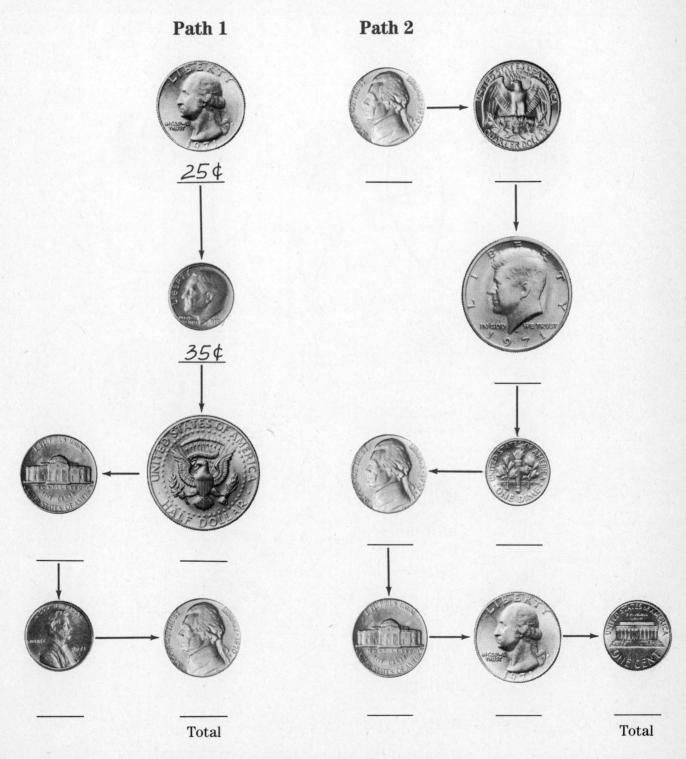

_25¢_

_35¢_

Total   Total

Total Sum (Path 1 + Path 2) _____

Money Circles

Add the coins in the circles that overlap. Write the sums in the blanks where the circles overlap. Then add together all the coins on the page. Write this sum at the bottom of the page.

Total sum of all the coins _____

Which Is Worth More?

There are two groups of coins in each of these exercises.
One group is worth more money than the other group.
Make an X under the group worth more money in each
exercise.

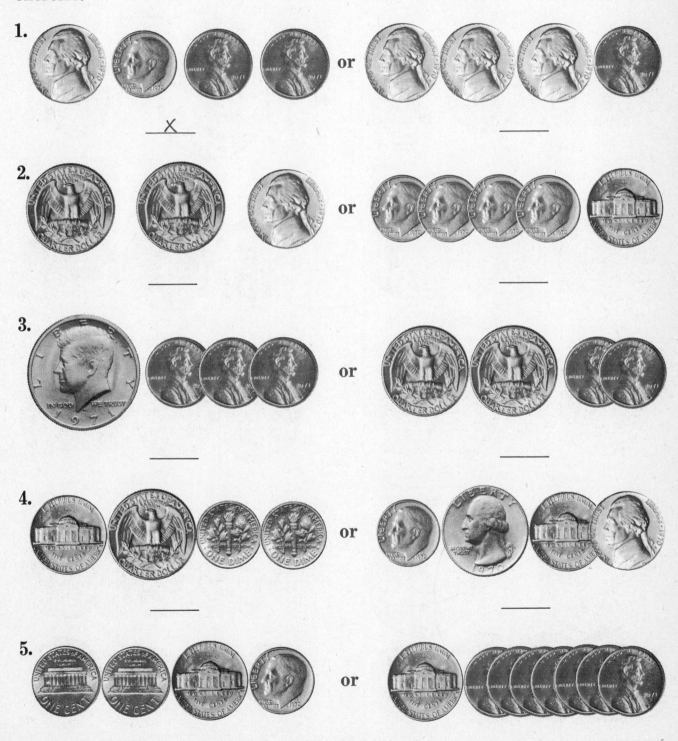

1.   or

     X   _____

2.   or

     _____   _____

3.   or

     _____   _____

4.   or

     _____   _____

5.   or

     _____   _____

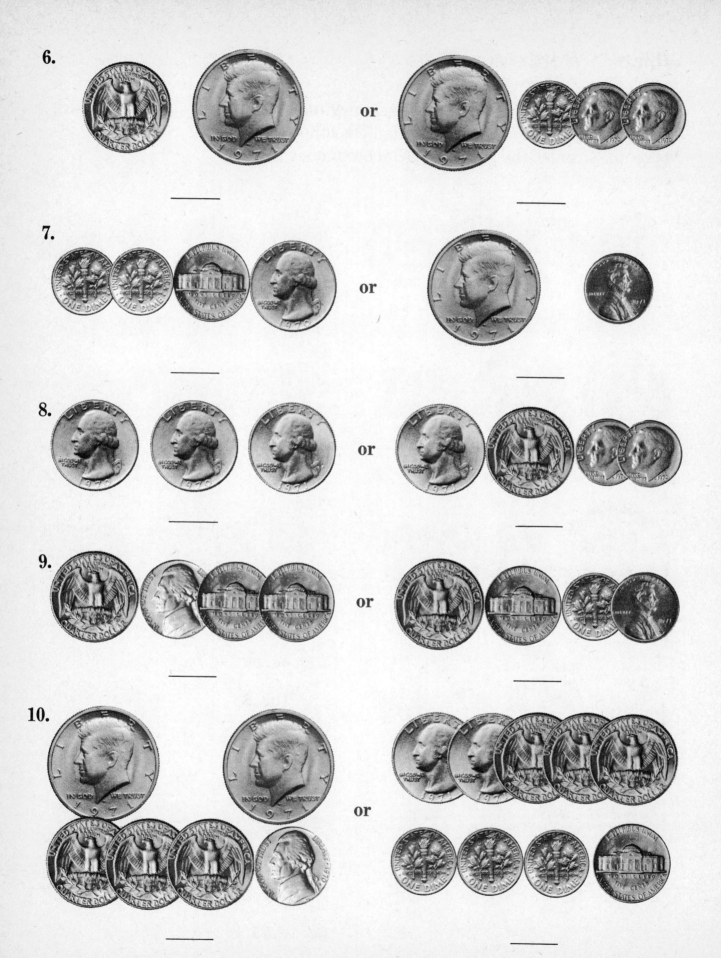

6. _____ or _____

7. _____ or _____

8. _____ or _____

9. _____ or _____

10. _____ or _____

Which Is Worth More?

There are two different amounts of money in each of
these exercises. Make an X in the blank following the
amount worth more money in each exercise.

1. 10¢, 25¢, 1¢, 5¢ ____ 25¢, 25¢ ___X___

2. 5¢, 10¢, 1¢, 1¢ ____ 1¢, 1¢, 5¢, 5¢, 1¢ ____

3. 25¢, 50¢, 10¢, 5¢ ____ 50¢, 10¢, 10¢, 10¢, 5¢ ____

4. 1¢, 1¢, 1¢, 10¢ ____ 5¢, 5¢, 5¢ ____

5. 50¢, 25¢ ____ 25¢, 25¢, 10¢, 10¢ ____

6. 25¢, 25¢, 5¢ ____ 10¢, 10¢, 10¢, 10¢ ____

7. 5¢, 10¢, 25¢ ____ 10¢, 50¢, 1¢ ____

8. $1, 10¢, 5¢, 1¢ ____ $1, 5¢, 5¢, 1¢, 1¢ ____

9. 25¢, 50¢, 5¢, 5¢ ____ 5¢, 10¢, 25¢, 50¢ ____

10. 50¢, $1, 1¢, 1¢ ____ 25¢, 25¢, 1¢, $1 ____

11. 10¢, 10¢, 10¢, 10¢ ____ 10¢, 10¢, 5¢, 5¢, 5¢ ____

12. 50¢, 10¢, 5¢, $1 ____ $1, 5¢, 10¢, 10¢, 25¢ ____

13. 25¢, 10¢, 25¢, 5¢ ____ 10¢, 5¢, 5¢, 5¢, 5¢ ____

14. 25¢, $1, $1, 1¢ ____ 10¢, 10¢, $1, $1, 5¢ ____

15. 10¢, 25¢, 50¢, 5¢ ____ 25¢, 25¢, 25¢, 10¢ ____

16. 5¢, 5¢, 5¢, 5¢, $1 ____ 5¢, $1, 1¢, 10¢, 10¢ ____

17. $1, $1, 10¢, 10¢, 5¢ ____ 5¢, 50¢, 50¢, 25¢, $1 ____

18. 5¢, 50¢, 50¢, 50¢ ____ 25¢, 25¢, 50¢, 50¢, 10¢ ____

19. 50¢, $1, $1, 1¢ ____ 25¢, 25¢, 50¢, 50¢, $1 ____

20. $1, $1, 50¢ ____ 5¢, 1¢, $1, $1, $1 ____

The Coin Wheel

Count the coins between the spokes of the wheel.
Start with the center coin each time and work out to the rim of the wheel.
Write the totals in the blanks along the rim.

Total 33¢

Total___

Total___

Total___

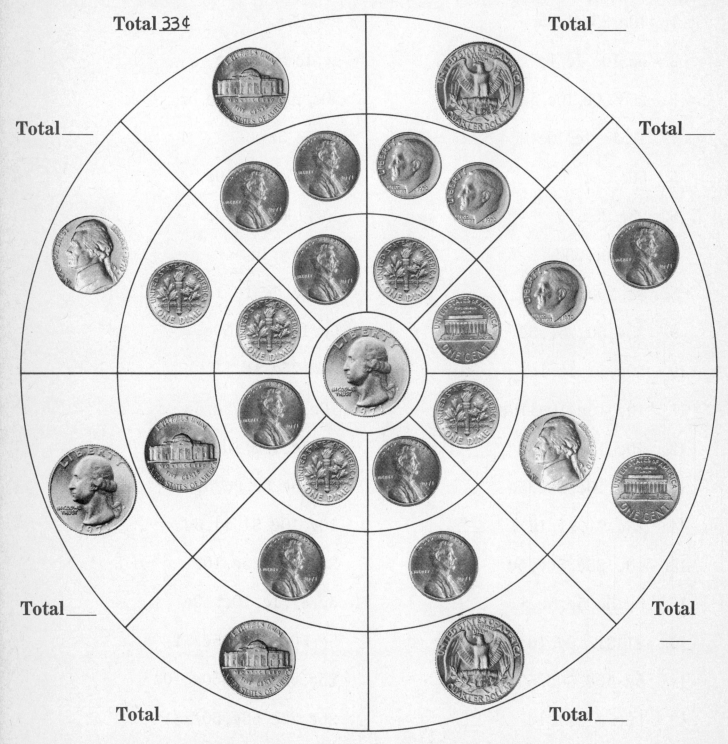

Total___

Total
___

Total___

Total___

Add the totals around the rim of the wheel. What is the sum? _____

NAME _____

Which Is Worth More?

Each of these exercises shows two amounts of money.
If the money on the left is worth more, write L in the
blank. If the money on the right is worth more, write R
in the blank.

1.

_R_

2.

____

3.

____

4.

____

5.

____

6.

——

7.

——

8.

——

9.

——

10.

——

Which Is Worth More?

Draw a line under the larger amount of money in each exercise.

1.	<u>8 pennies, 2 dimes</u>	1 quarter, 2 pennies
2.	2 dimes, 5 pennies	1 quarter, 1 dime
3.	6 nickels, 12 pennies	6 dimes, 7 pennies
4.	2 dimes, 5 nickels	2 quarters
5.	1 half-dollar	1 nickel, 4 dimes
6.	7 dimes, 2 pennies	1 half-dollar, 1 dime
7.	4 quarters, 3 nickels	9 dimes, 9 pennies
8.	1 half-dollar, 1 dime	2 quarters, 3 nickels
9.	8 dimes, 2 pennies	3 quarters, 2 nickels
10.	2 half-dollars	3 quarters, 2 dimes
11.	2 dollars, 2 dimes	3 half-dollars, 2 quarters
12.	4 dimes, 3 pennies	6 nickels, 1 dime
13.	1 dollar	4 quarters, 3 dimes
14.	5 quarters, 2 nickels	1 dollar, 6 nickels
15.	8 dimes, 1 quarter	2 half-dollars

The Money Maze

Count each line of coins from the center out. Write the
totals in the answer boxes.

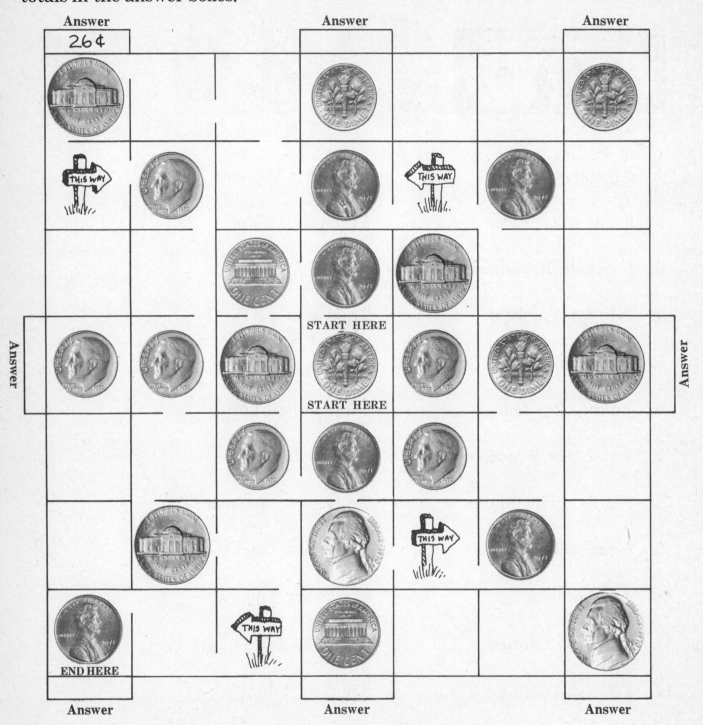

Now, to go through the maze, start in the center and
follow the openings through each square. Add each coin
as you pass through the maze. Write the total value
here: _____

NAME _____

Place in Order

Arrange the amounts of money in order from the
smallest to the largest. Write them in order in the blanks
using numbers, the dollar sign, and a decimal point.

1. eight cents   five cents
    fourteen cents   twelve cents

    $.05 $.08 $.12 $.14

2. forty-two cents   ten cents
    eleven cents   two cents
    fifteen cents

    ____ ____ ____ ____ ____

3. eighteen cents   one cent
    eighty cents   thirteen cents
    seven cents

    ____ ____ ____ ____ ____

4. nineteen cents   two cents
    forty-one cents   sixty cents
    eighteen cents

    ____ ____ ____ ____ ____

5. one dollar   thirty cents
    fourteen cents   two cents
    ninety cents

    ____ ____ ____ ____ ____

6. fifty cents   eighty-eight cents
    one cent   one dollar
    seventy cents

    ____ ____ ____ ____ ____

7. three dollars   ten cents
    twenty cents   six dollars
    four dollars

    ____ ____ ____ ____ ____

8. eighty-nine cents   two dollars
    fifty-one cents   forty-eight cents

    ____ ____ ____ ____

9. one dollar and fifty cents
    three dollars and thirty cents
    seventy-five cents
    two dollars and thirty cents
    two dollars

    ____ ____ ____ ____ ____

10. four dollars and thirty-two cents
    two dollars and ten cents
    four dollars and seventy-one cents
    one dollar and five cents
    three dollars

    ____ ____ ____ ____ ____

Arrange the amounts of money in order from the
smallest to the largest. Write them in order in the blanks
using words.

11. 18¢   3¢   36¢   54¢   **12.** 16¢   86¢   92¢   37¢

_____three   cents_____   _____

_____eighteen   cents_____   _____

_____thirty-six   cents_____   _____

_____fifty-four   cents_____   _____

13. 11¢   8¢   14¢   3¢   24¢   **14.** 30¢   70¢   40¢   90¢   12¢

_____   _____

_____   _____

_____   _____

_____   _____

_____   _____

15. 19¢   73¢   70¢   74¢ $1.00   **16.** 44¢ $2   20¢   22¢ $2.20

_____   _____

_____   _____

_____   _____

_____   _____

NAME _____

Place in Order

Arrange the amounts of money in order from the
smallest to the largest. Write them in order in the
blanks, using numbers. Use the dollar sign and decimal
point for amounts over a dollar, and the cents sign for
amounts under a dollar.

1. two dimes and one nickel
    three dimes
    one quarter and two pennies
    one dime and two nickels

    _20¢_ _25¢_ _27¢_ _30¢_

2. four dimes
    one quarter and two dimes
    one quarter, one dime, and
       one penny
    two dimes and three nickels

    ____ ____ ____ ____

3. two quarters, one dime, and
       one nickel
    three quarters
    one quarter and three dimes
    one half-dollar

    ____ ____ ____ ____

4. one dime and three nickels
    nineteen pennies
    one dime and ten pennies
    five nickels and one penny

    ____ ____ ____ ____

5. six dimes
    six nickels
    five quarters
    one half-dollar and two quarters

    ____ ____ ____ ____

6. three quarters and two dimes
    one half-dollar and four dimes
    two quarters and four nickels
    three quarters and ten pennies

    ____ ____ ____ ____

7. four quarters and one nickel
    one half-dollar and three
       quarters
    one dollar, one dime, and one
       nickel
    one half-dollar and six dimes

    ____ ____ ____ ____

8. two half-dollars and three dimes
    one dollar and two quarters
    one dollar and four nickels
    one half-dollar and fifty pennies

    ____ ____ ____ ____

Coin Clusters

Add the coins connected by lines. Write the totals in the blanks in the center. Then put the totals in order from the smallest amount to the largest. Write these totals at the bottom of the page.

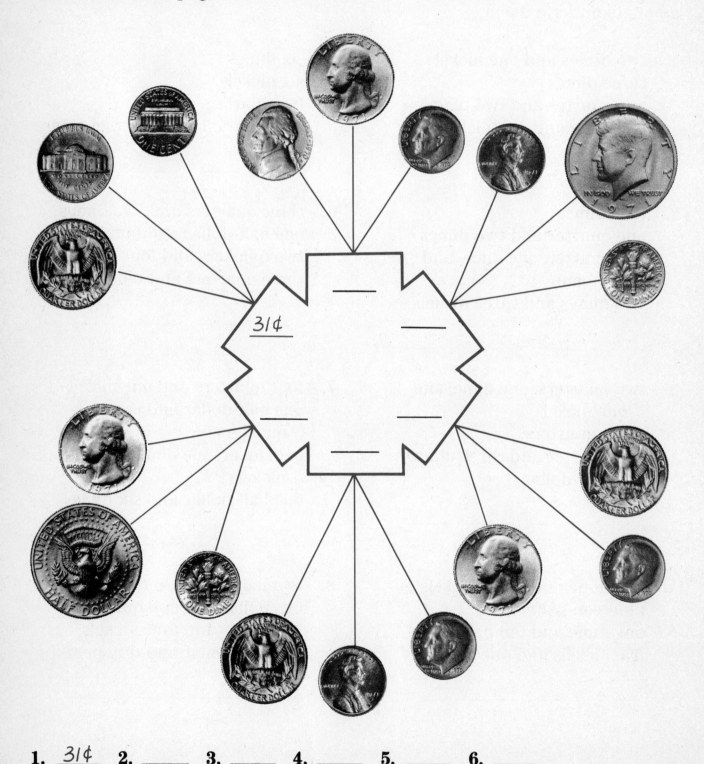

1. __31¢__ 2. _____ 3. _____ 4. _____ 5. _____ 6. _____

NAME _____

Which Coin Is Missing?

Write the correct amount on the blank coin to make the
total value of the coins equal to the amount on the right.

1.  = 64¢

2.  = $1

3.  = 19¢

4.  = 93¢

5.  = 67¢

6.  = 40¢

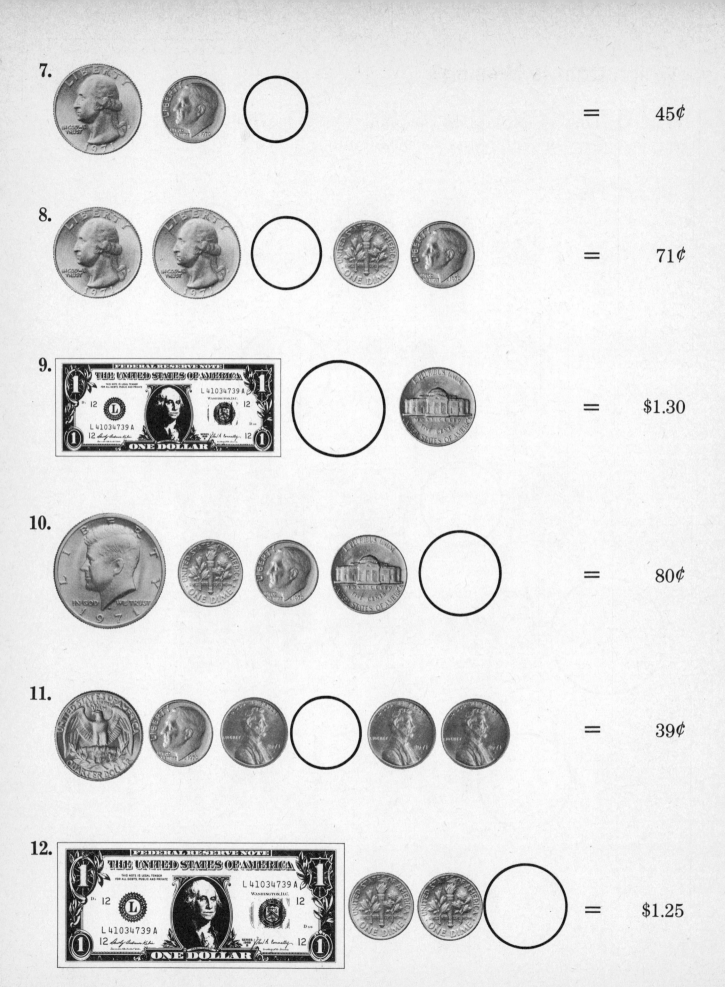

7.   =   45¢

8.   =   71¢

9.   = $1.30

10. =   80¢

11. =   39¢

12. = $1.25

NAME _____

Which Coins Are Missing?

Write the correct amounts on the blank coins to make the
total value of the coins equal to the amount on the right.

1. 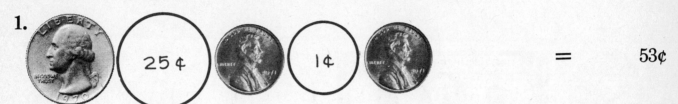 = 53¢

2.  = 55¢

3.  = 51¢

4.  = 46¢

5.  = 82¢

6.  = 81¢

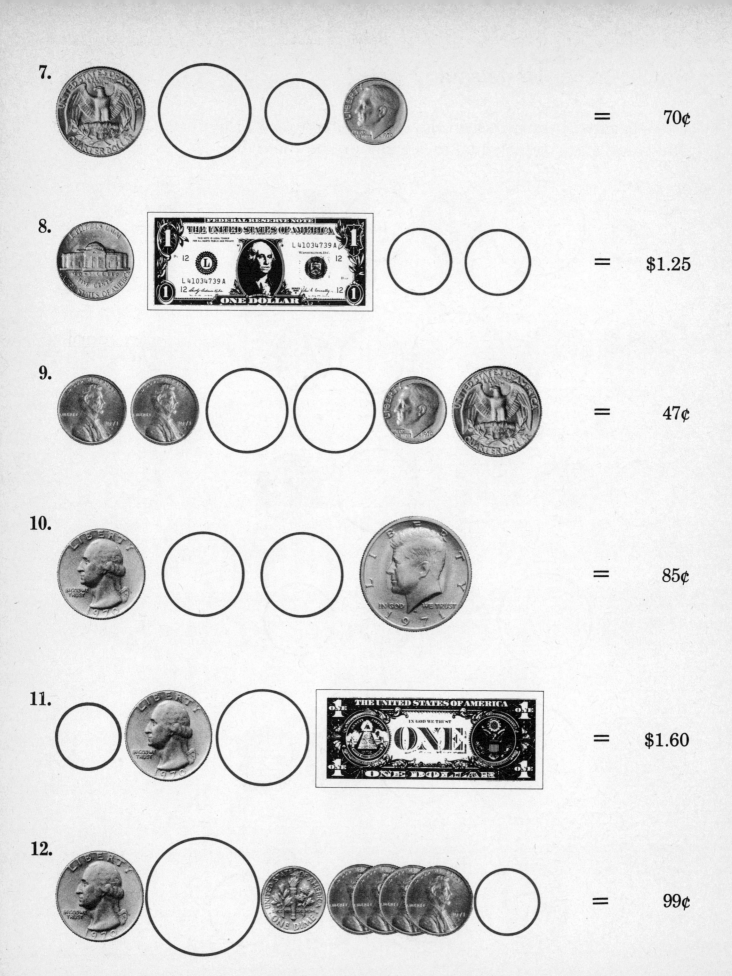

7. $\bigcirc$ $\bigcirc$ $\bigcirc$ $\bigcirc$ = 70¢

8. $\bigcirc$ $\bigcirc$ $\bigcirc$ $\bigcirc$ = $1.25

9. $\bigcirc$ $\bigcirc$ $\bigcirc$ $\bigcirc$ $\bigcirc$ $\bigcirc$ = 47¢

10. $\bigcirc$ $\bigcirc$ $\bigcirc$ $\bigcirc$ = 85¢

11. $\bigcirc$ $\bigcirc$ $\bigcirc$ $\bigcirc$ = $1.60

12. $\bigcirc$ $\bigcirc$ $\bigcirc$ $\bigcirc$ $\bigcirc$ $\bigcirc$ $\bigcirc$ = 99¢

NAME _____

How Much Is It?

Write in the blanks the total value of the coins and bills on the left.
Choose your answers from this list:

ninety-five cents   fifty-five cents   thirty-two cents
sixteen cents   sixty-two cents   two dollars
one dollar   fifty-nine cents   ninety cents

1.

sixteen cents

2.

_____

3.

_____

4.

_____

5.

_____

6.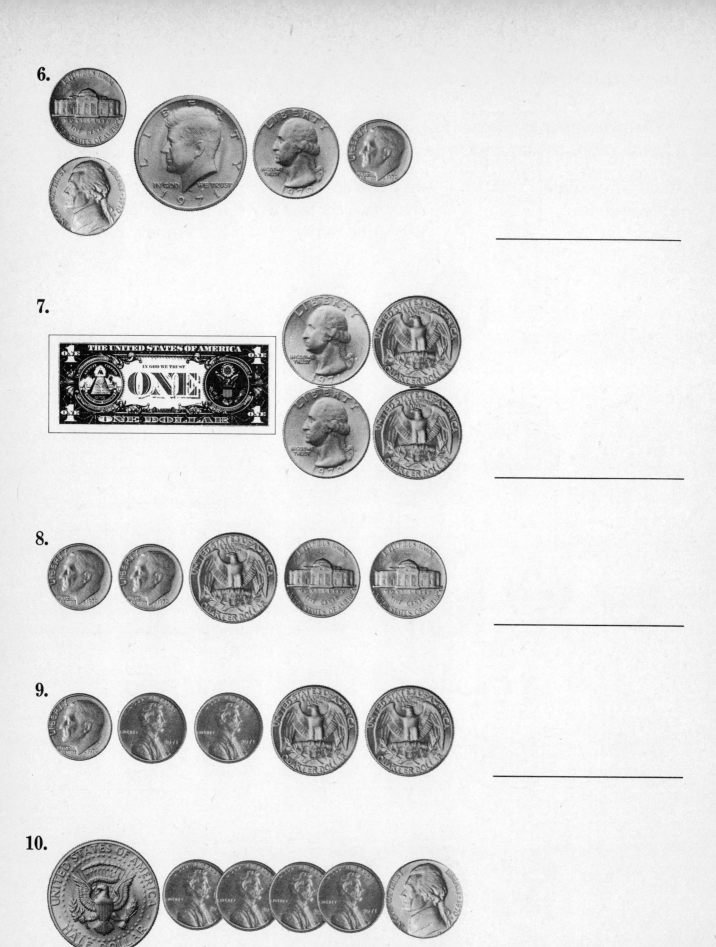

_____

7.

_____

8.

_____

9.

_____

10.

_____

NAME _____

How Much Is It?

Write in the blanks the total value of the coins and bills
on the left. Use numbers.

1.  $ .35

2.  $ _____

3.  $ _____

4.  $ _____

5.  $ _____

6.  $ _____

7.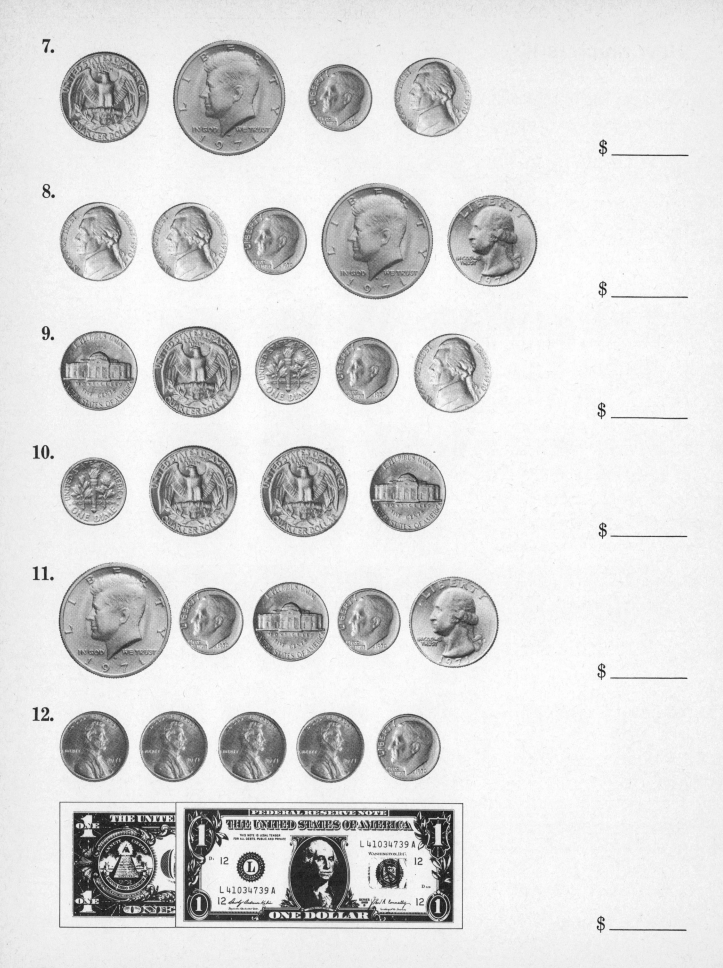

$ _____

8.

$ _____

9.

$ _____

10.

$ _____

11.

$ _____

12.

$ _____

How Much Is It?

Write in the blanks the total value of the coins and bills on the left. Use numbers.

1.

$ _3.40_

2.

$ ___.___

3.

$ ___.___

4.

$ ___.___

5.

$ ___.___

The Money Wheel

Add the money connected by lines. Write the sums in the circles. Then add the sums to get the total value of the money wheel.

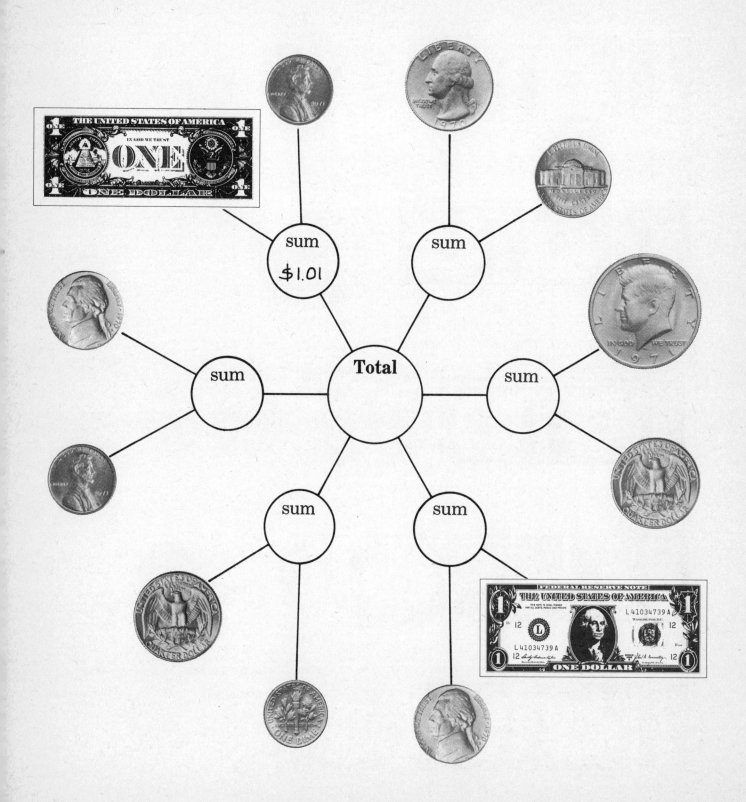

How Much Is It?

Write in the blanks the total value of the money on the left.
Use numbers.

1. 5 dollars, 1 quarter, and 2 dimes $ <u>5.45</u>

2. 3 half-dollars, 4 dimes, and 6 pennies $ __.___

3. 4 quarters, 8 nickels, and 3 pennies $ __.___

4. 20 dimes, 3 quarters, and 3 nickels $ __.___

5. 4 dollars, 2 half-dollars, and 1 dime $ __.___

6. 8 quarters, 4 nickels, and 15 pennies $ __.___

7. 7 dollars, 1 half-dollar, and 1 quarter $ __.___

8. 5 quarters, 4 dimes, and 3 nickels $ __.___

9. 6 dollars, 1 quarter, and 10 nickels $ __.___

10. 4 half-dollars, 2 dimes, and 2 nickels $ __.___

11. 8 dollars, 2 half-dollars, and 9 pennies $ __.___

12. 5 dollars, 4 half-dollars, and 7 nickels $ __.___

13. 30 dimes, 20 nickels, and 13 pennies $ __.___

14. 6 dollars, 2 quarters, 1 nickel, and 1 penny $ __.___

15. 8 half-dollars, 3 dimes, and 6 nickels $ __.___

16. 7 quarters, 1 half-dollar, and 7 pennies $ __.___

17. 5 half-dollars, 1 dime, 1 nickel, and 8 pennies $ __.___

18. 7 dollars, 5 quarters, and 5 nickels $ __.___

19. 3 dollars, 4 half-dollars, 4 quarters, and 10 dimes $ __.___

20. 9 dollars, 3 quarters, 2 dimes, and 4 pennies $ __.___

21. 2 dollars, 3 quarters, and 1 dime   = $2.85

22. 1 dollar, 4 dimes, and 3 nickels   = $___.___

23. 6 dollars and 5 quarters   = $___.___

24. 1 dollar, 3 half-dollars, and 3 nickels = $___.___

25. 2 half-dollars, 3 quarters, and 15 pennies = $___.___

26. 4 dollars, 4 quarters, and 4 dimes   = $___.___

27. 10 dimes, 4 nickels, and 7 pennies   = $___.___

28. 7 dollars, 3 quarters, and 3 dimes   = $___.___

29. 9 dollars, 6 nickels, and 4 pennies   = $___.___

30. 11 dimes, 2 nickels, and 6 pennies   = $___.___

31. 5 quarters, 4 dimes, and 2 nickels   = $___.___

32. 3 dollars, 2 half-dollars, and 4 quarters = $___.___

33. 2 dollars, 6 quarters, and 6 dimes   = $___.___

34. 8 dollars, 1 half-dollar, and 3 quarters = $___.___

35. 3 half-dollars, 4 dimes, and 4 nickels   = $___.___

36. 8 dollars, 2 quarters, and 3 dimes   = $___.___

37. 6 quarters, 3 dimes, and 3 nickels   = $___.___

38. 5 dollars, 5 quarters, and 1 nickel   = $___.___

39. 3 dollars, 3 quarters, and 4 dimes   = $___.___

40. 7 dollars, 3 quarters, and 2 pennies   = $___.___

How Many Are There?

Fill in the blanks on the right with the number of coins
or bills needed to make the amount on the left.

1. $2.15 = __2__ dollars, __1__ dime, and __5__ pennies

2. $3.76 = _____ dollars, _____ quarters, and _____ penny

3. $3.50 = _____ half-dollars

4. $6.35 = _____ dollars and _____ nickels

5. $5.83 = _____ dollars, _____ dimes, and _____ pennies

6. $2.25 = _____ quarters

7. $1.10 = _____ dimes

8. $7.48 = _____ dollars, _____ dimes, and _____ pennies

9. $4.56 = _____ dollars, _____ half-dollar, and _____ pennies

10. $8.95 = _____ dollars, _____ quarters, and _____ nickels

11. $5.07 = _____ dollars, _____ nickel, and _____ pennies

12. $ .82 = _____ quarters and _____ pennies

13. $1.59 = _____ dimes, _____ nickel, and _____ pennies

14. $6.22 = _____ dollars, _____ nickels, and _____ pennies

15. $9.70 = _____ dollars, _____ quarters, and _____ dimes

16. $4.35 = _____ half-dollars and _____ nickels

17. $7.45 = _____ dollars, _____ quarter, and _____ dimes

18. $3.33 = _____ dollars, _____ dimes, and _____ pennies

19. $8.85 = _____ dollars, _____ quarters, and _____ nickels

20. $9.19 = _____ dollars, _____ nickels, and _____ pennies

21. $1.85 = __1__ dollar, __3__ quarters, and __1__ dime

22. $2.22 = _____ dollars, _____ dimes, and _____ pennies

23. $5.25 = _____ dollars and _____ nickels

24. $4.27 = _____ dollars, _____ quarter, and _____ pennies

25. $2.00 = _____ quarters

26. $5.56 = _____ dollars, _____ quarters, and _____ pennies

27. $1.30 = _____ quarters and _____ nickel

28. $7.29 = _____ dollars, _____ nickels, and _____ pennies

29. $ .95 = _____ half-dollar, _____ quarter, and _____ dimes

30. $6.33 = _____ dollars, _____ dimes, and _____ pennies

31. $2.10 = _____ quarters and _____ dime

32. $6.97 = _____ dollars, _____ dimes, and _____ pennies

33. $4.65 = _____ dollars, _____ quarters, and _____ nickels

34. $1.80 = _____ half-dollars, _____ quarters, and _____ dimes

35. $3.70 = _____ dollars, _____ quarters, and _____ nickels

36. $ .80 = _____ quarters and _____ dimes

37. $8.17 = _____ dollars, _____ dime, and _____ pennies

38. $7.31 = _____ dollars, _____ dimes, and _____ penny

39. $2.25 = _____ dollar, _____ half-dollars, and _____ quarter

40. $7.77 = _____ dollars, _____ dimes, and _____ pennies

Coin Questions

Here are some questions about coins. Think about each
question before you write your answer in the blank.

1. What 4 coins equal one dollar? _____ 4 quarters _____

2. What 5 coins equal a quarter? _____

3. What 3 coins equal 25¢? _____

4. What 6 coins equal thirty cents? _____

5. What 7 coins equal 45¢? _____

6. What 5 coins equal eighty-five cents? _____

    _____

7. What 7 coins equal 75¢? _____

    _____

8. What 3 coins equal $1.00? _____

    _____

9. What 8 coins equal $1.05? _____

    _____

10. What 6 coins equal $1.22? _____

    _____

11. What 8 coins equal 75¢? _____

_____

12. What 9 coins equal 87¢? _____

_____

13. What 8 coins equal $2.25? _____

_____

14. What 8 coins equal $2.50? _____

_____

15. What 7 coins equal 90¢? _____

_____

16. What 10 coins equal $1.82? _____

_____

17. What 8 coins equal $1.56? _____

_____

18. What 9 coins equal $2.25? _____

_____

19. What 9 coins equal $1.06? _____

_____

20. What 8 coins equal 99¢? _____

_____

21. What bill and coin equal $1.50? _____

_____

22. What bill and 5 coins equal $2.25? _____

_____

Telephone Quiz

When you make a call on a pay telephone, you use coins. The coins you use are the quarter, the dime, and the nickel. The telephone operator will tell you how much money to deposit. Follow the telephone operator's instructions in each of these problems. Make X's under the coins you must deposit for your call.

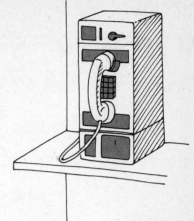

1. On your call to Tampa, deposit 55¢, please.

     X   ___   X   X   ___   ___

2. On your call to San Francisco, deposit 25¢, please.

   ___   ___   ___   ___   ___   ___

3. On your call to El Paso, deposit 85¢, please.

   ___   ___   ___   ___   ___   ___

4. On your call to Mobile, deposit $1.15, please.

5. On your call to New York, deposit 95¢, please.

——— ——— ——— ——— ——— ——— ———

6. On your call to Baltimore, deposit 40¢, please.

——— ——— ——— ——— ——— ———

7. On your call to Philadelphia, deposit 80¢, please.

——— ——— ——— ——— ——— ——— ———

8. On your call to Denver, deposit $1.00, please.

——— ——— ——— ——— ——— ——— ———

9. On your call to Chicago, deposit 90¢, please.

——— ——— ——— ——— ——— ——— ——— ———

10. On your call to Los Angeles, deposit 65¢, please.

——— ——— ——— ——— ——— ——— ———

Shopping Quiz

These items are found in a grocery store.

79¢   72¢   87¢   63¢

82¢   83¢   44¢   92¢

Show that you know how to use coins. Make an X under the item that costs as much as the coins on the left.

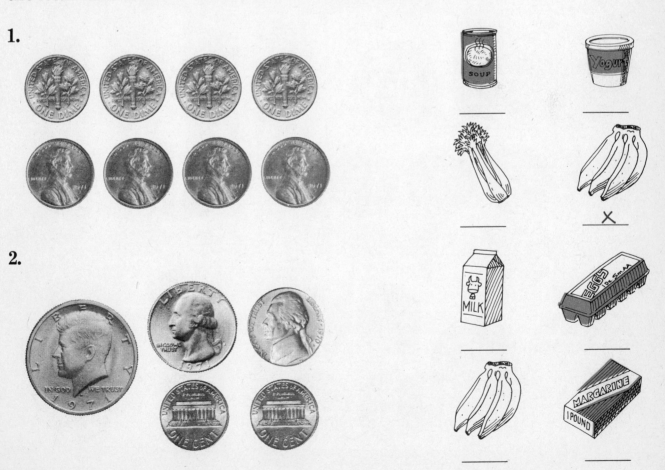

1.

2.

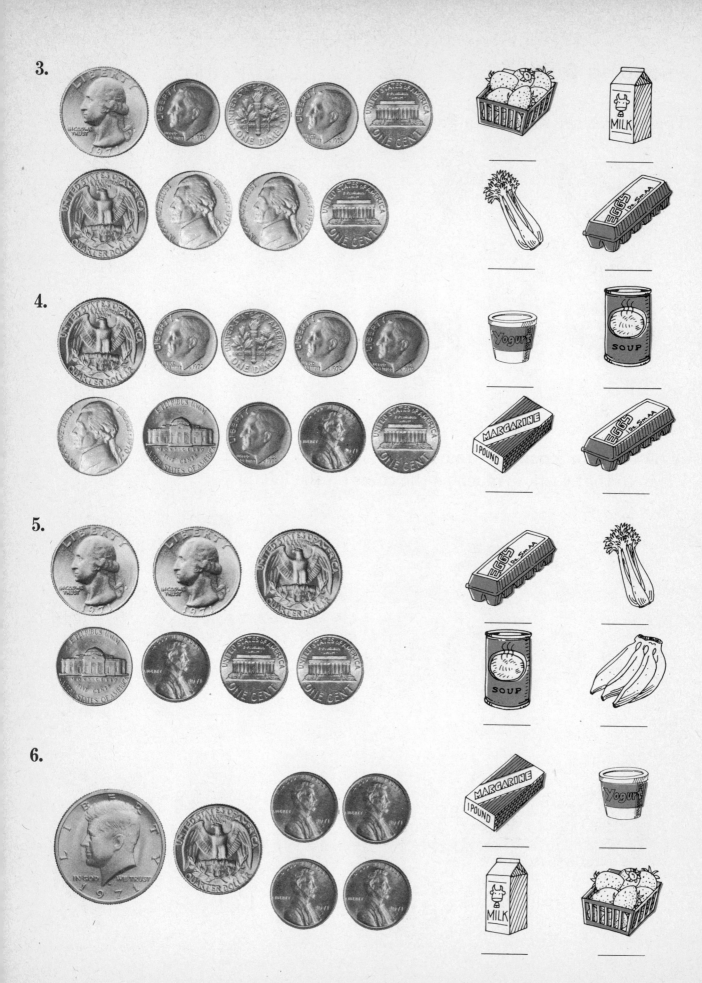

3.

4.

5.

6.

Shopping Quiz

These items are found in a drugstore.

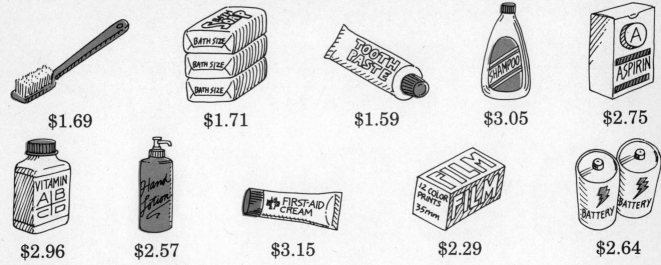

$1.69 $1.71 $1.59 $3.05 $2.75

$2.96 $2.57 $3.15 $2.29 $2.64

Show that you know how to use money. Make an X under the item that costs as much as the money on the left.

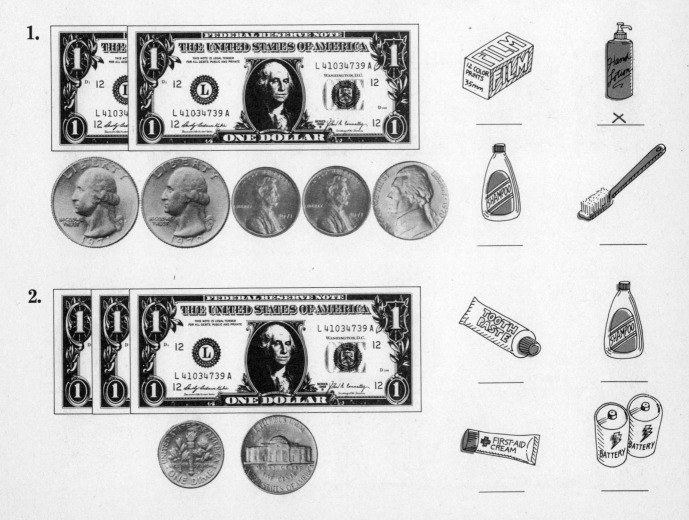

3.

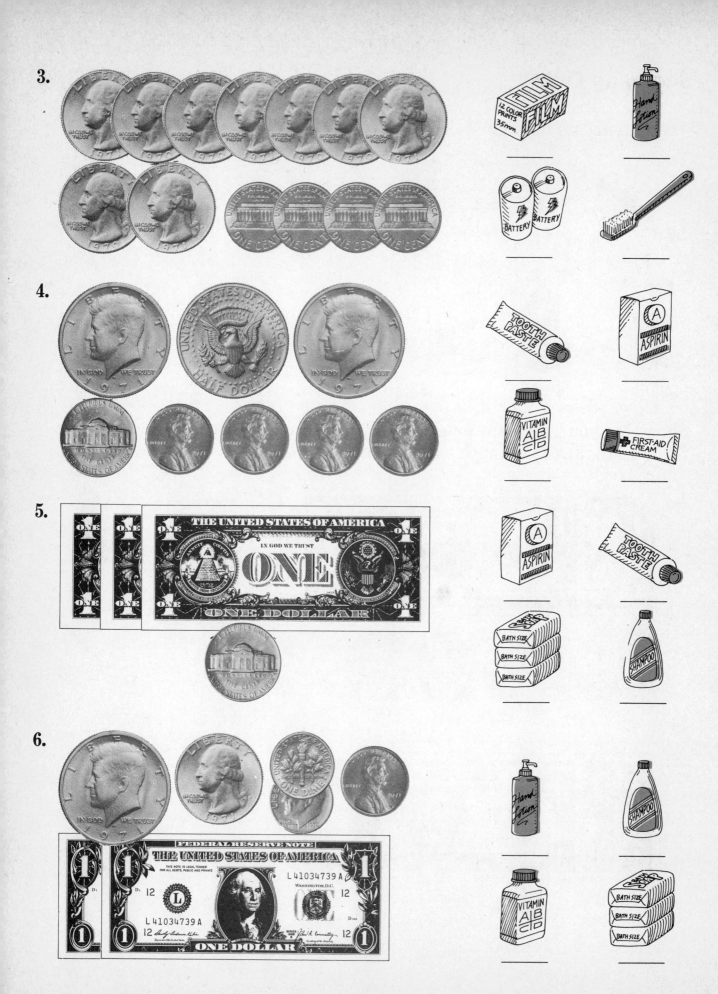

6.

Shopping Quiz

These items are found in a hardware store.

$1.35 $2.45 $3.42 $3.59

$4.45 $5.79 $4.52 $4.25

Show that you know how to use money. Make an X under
the item that costs as much as the money on the left.

1.

2.

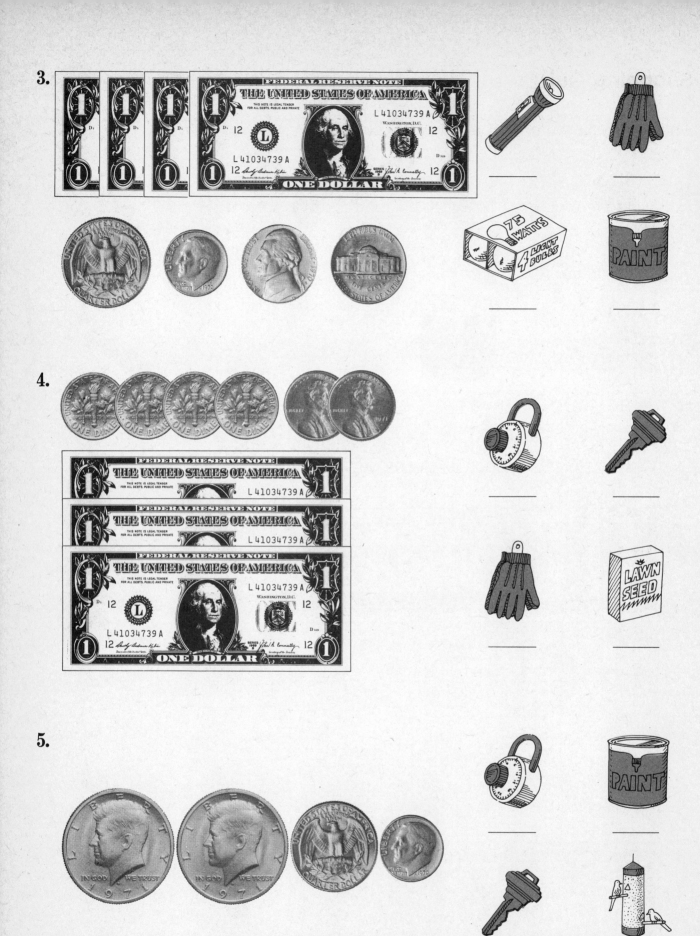

3.

——— ———

——— ———

4.

——— ———

——— ———

5.

——— ———

——— ———

Shopping Quiz

These items are found in a clothing store.

$1.50 $5.35 $5.75 $4.65

$4.95 $9.00 $8.35 $8.50

Show that you know how to use money. Make an X under the item that costs as much as the money on the left.

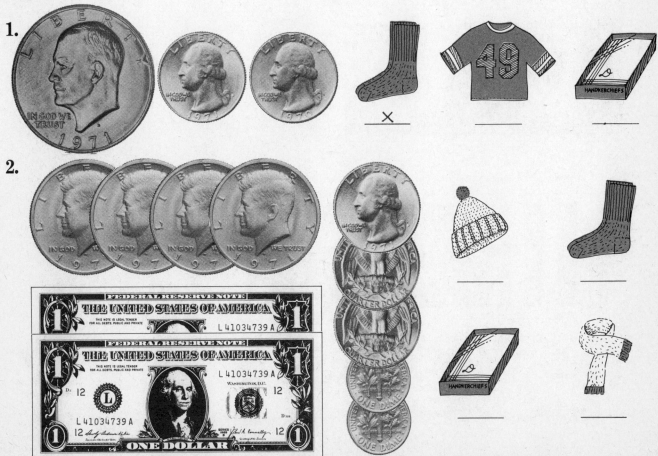

1.

2.

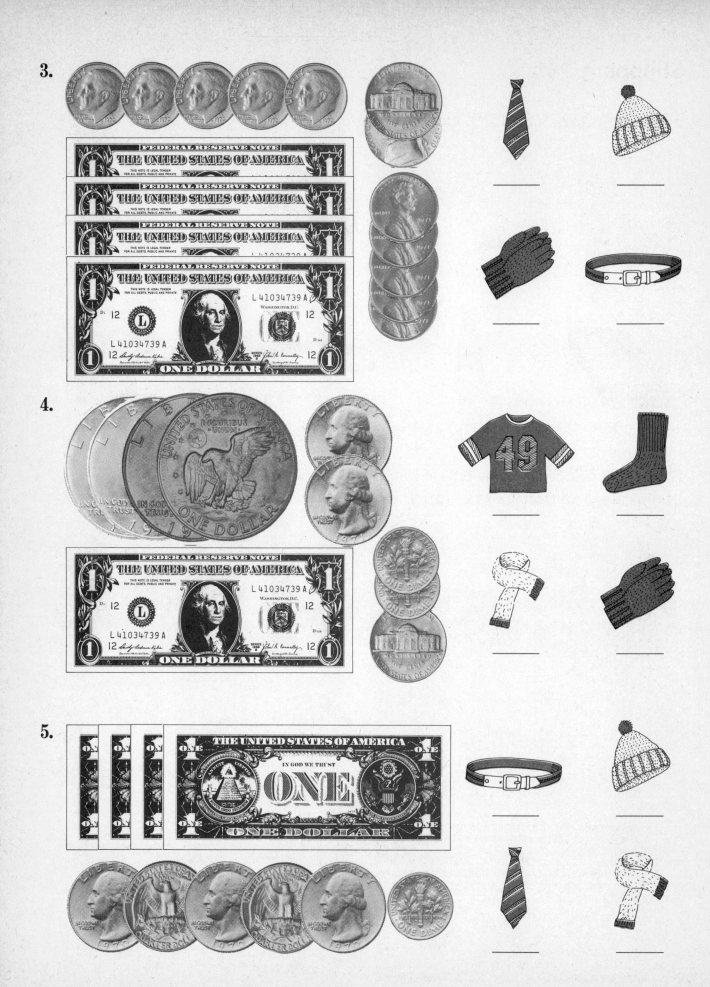

3.

4.

5.

Shopping Quiz

The items at the right are found in a bookstore. Make X's
under the coins and bills you would use to pay for these items.

1.

$4.60

X X X X ___ ___

X X ___ X ___

2.

$2.25

___ ___ ___

___ ___ ___

3.

$3.45

4.

$3.40

_____ _____ _____

_____ _____ _____

5.

$4.65

_____ _____ _____

_____ _____ _____

6.

$5.55

_____ _____ _____

_____ _____ _____

Posttest I

NAME _____

In these exercises, you are buying different things in a store. Make an X under each item that costs as much as the money below the items.

1.

X _____ _____ _____

 ...

2.

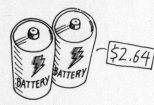 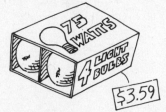  

_____ _____ _____ _____

3.

_____ _____ _____ _____

4.

 95¢

 $1.50

 $1.35

 $1.69

_____

5.

 $4.45

 $5.55

 $5.35

 $7.50

_____

6.

 $4.65

 $2.96

 $.97

 $3.15

_____

Posttest II

In these exercises, you are buying different things in
a store. Make X's under the coins and bills you will use
to pay for what you buy.

1. You are buying $ .67

   You pay with

   X   X   X   X   X   X

2. You are buying $ .92

   You pay with

3. You are buying $2.29

   You pay with

4. You are buying  $2.96

You pay with

_____ _____ _____ _____ _____ _____ _____

_____

5. You are buying $ .63

You pay with

_____ _____ _____ _____ _____ _____ _____ _____

6. You are buying $1.50

You pay with

_____ _____ _____ _____ _____ _____ _____